DYNAMIC INDUCTION

DYNAMIC INDUCTION

Games, Activities and Ideas to Revitalize Your Employee Induction Process

SUSAN EL-SHAMY

Routledge
Taylor & Francis Group

LONDON AND NEW YORK

First published in paperback 2024

First published 2003 by Gower Publishing

Published 2016
by Routledge
4 Park Square, Milton Park, Abingdon, Oxon OX14 4RN

and by Routledge
605 Third Avenue, New York, NY 10158

Routledge is an imprint of the Taylor & Francis Group, an informa business

British Library Cataloguing in Publication Data

El-Shamy, Susan
   Induction instruction: games for induction training
   1. Employee orientation 2. Educational games
   I. Title
   658.3′1242

   ISBN 978 0 566 08544 4

Library of Congress Control Number: 2003106747

ISBN: 978-0-566-08544-4 (hbk)
ISBN: 978-1-03-283761-1 (pbk)
ISBN: 978-1-315-57830-9 (ebk)

DOI: 10.4324/9781315578309

Typeset by MHL Typesetting Limited, Coventry.

Contents

Contents

Introduction

Endless windows of opportunity slide through the early workdays of every new employee: arriving for the first day of work; meeting new work colleagues; entering the workplace for the first time; trying to find the photocopier; filling in benefit forms; attending a staff meeting. These are all opportunities for creating positive impressions, instilling comfort and confidence, learning how things are done and shaping perceptions and attitudes. If left to chance, these opportunities may be missed or worse, they may be filled with experiences that do more harm than good. Having a dynamic employee induction process is all about taking advantage of these opportunities to enable the new employee to become a positive, productive member of the organization as quickly as possible. A dynamic induction process is active and vibrant. It does not wait and watch and hope for the best. It immediately involves and engages the new employee, from the moment they sign the contract and throughout their early hours, days, weeks and months on the job.

A dynamic induction process involves not only new employees, but supervisors, co-workers and other key colleagues in the organization. All work together to welcome new employees, integrate them into the workplace, facilitate their learning and help solve problems that might arise. During this dynamic process, communication is increased, cooperation is enhanced and group cohesiveness is improved. This book is all about how you can revitalize your employee induction programme, take advantage of those many windows of opportunity and speed the assimilation of new employees into your organization.

About this Book

Dynamic Induction is a practical guide to up-grading your employee induction process. It is designed to make it as easy as possible for you to take action and repair, revitalize, or even rebuild your entire attitude to new employees and their assimilation procedure. In a compact series of assessments, quizzes, charts and checklists, this book presents more than 200 ideas and suggestions for enhancing and energizing your complete induction process beginning the moment a new employee accepts the job. *Dynamic Induction* also provides you with 50 games and structured activities that can be used to impart work-related information to people embarking on a new job. These games and activities can be used in all the instruction-related aspects of your induction process, including planned actions taken to welcome and help the new person, as well as specific learning events designed to accelerate the integration of the new employee into the workforce.

Part One – The Induction Process

Part One of *Dynamic Induction* begins with an overview of what a dynamic induction process is, including reasons for having such a process, the reasons people give for not having one and a short true-or-false test of your own ideas about induction. There is also an induction process assessment that will let you determine the improvements needed for various aspects of your organization's induction process. Part One then presents five instructional areas within the induction process: pre-induction activities; the first hour, day, week and month of the new employee; induction training programmes; induction companion programmes; and induction printed and electronic media. General information is presented for each area, as well as various charts, checklists and practical suggestions on improving that particular area of induction. Each of these five sections ends with a list of games and activities from Part Two that could be used in that particular instructional area and an 'improvement project form' complete with a 'to-do list' so that you can immediately make notes about the improvements that you want to make.

Part Two – Dynamic Induction Games and Activities

The second part of the book contains 50 games and activities that can be used to energize and revitalize your induction process. In a dynamic induction process, games and activities are used in all facets of the process, including planned actions that welcome and help the new person, as well as specific learning events. Many of the games and activities in Part Two have variations that can be used in pre-induction activities and in induction companion programmes. There are also a number of games and activities that can be adapted for use on induction websites.

The games are divided into three categories. The first category contains games and activities for inclusion. These consist of activities to help people get acquainted, warm-ups and ice breakers, and reassurance and initiation games and activities. The second category contains information-sharing games and activities. These include general information-sharing games and games that share specific information on topics such as compliance issues, staffing and human resources, organizational structure and culture, and career development. The final category has games and activities for starting a new job.

Each game is presented in the same format beginning with an overview that states the purpose of the game, provides a short summary of the game, lists the materials needed, gives the time required and a suggested number of participants. This overview is followed by a step-by-step list of what to do, including: steps to take before the game, possible opening lines to use, instructions for playing the game, guidelines for the game, suggested questions for the debriefing of the game, and points to bring forth in the debrief. Each game ends with suggested variations for that game. Some of the games list one-on-one variations that can be used in companion programmes and a number of the games also give electronic variations for use on induction websites. Many of the games are 'ready-to-go' and require little, if any, preparation. Others will need to be customized to your particular organization and situation. Many of the information-sharing games and activities will require your gathering the most pertinent information and manipulating it in some way – preparing a quiz, organizing a handout or making a list of situations. Handouts or worksheets accompany some of the games.

Whether you need to make a few repairs to your induction workshop, or completely to renovate your entire induction process, there are games and activities here that can help you do that. You will want to be careful not to overdo and add too many games and activities, but one or two well-placed, enjoyable, energizing games can do wonders for any programme. Consider the overall design of your programme or workshop, the types of activities and events that occur. Look for lulls and periods of inactivity. Consider the length of time that participants are seated, the amount of time that they are passive recipients. Then add dynamic action, activity, and involvement where it is most needed. When you decide on a game or activity that you want to use, use it wholeheartedly. Make it as interesting and involving as possible. Try some accelerated learning techniques. Add music, colour, and inter-activity. Involve the participants in the process of learning. The dynamic results can be incredibly rewarding, for you as well as the participants!

How to Use This Book

Make dynamic use of this book. Actively and vigorously use it. Use it as a guide, a manual, a workbook. Write in it. Mark it up. Take the assessments. Underline and highlight things you want to do. Write in the margins. Use the Improvement Project Forms. Fill out the 'to do' lists. Develop your plans as you go. As you begin to implement your dynamic induction plans, come back to the book to check and evaluate how things are going. Come back to the book for another game, another activity, another idea to further improve and revitalize your induction process. Good luck.

PART ONE

The Induction Process

Introduction to the Induction Process

Employee induction is the act of installing a new employee into a position within an organization. It can refer to anything from a ten-minute 'welcome aboard' speech to a three-day training programme. The phrase 'induction process' refers to the on-going procedure of assisting a new employee to become a fully productive member of the organization's workforce. It is used for a longer-term progression of activities and events. Although the term 'employee orientation' can be used to refer to the launching of new employees into the workplace, it is more commonly used for a meeting or programme at which introductory information or training is provided. Such meetings or programmes are also called induction or orientation seminars, workshops and classes. The term 'induction', although in common usage in the UK and elsewhere, is rarely used in the United States; 'orientation' and the 'orientation process' are the common terms in the US.

While induction classes can be invaluable in integrating new employees into the organization, an induction process includes more than induction classes. An induction process extends through a longer period of time and covers more aspects of assimilating the new employee. A dynamic induction process is a vibrant, proactive process that covers all aspects of the induction process. It begins the moment the prospective new employee agrees to take the job. It includes actions taken before the employee begins their new job, often called pre-induction activities, and includes planned actions taken in the early minutes, days and weeks of the new person's employment as well. The dynamic induction process also includes orientation or induction training events, induction companion programmes and electronic and printed media used for conveying work-related information to all new employees.

A dynamic induction process is therefore more thorough and effective than any single programme. By extending over a longer period of time, a dynamic induction process can address a wider variety of issues, involve more people, and build added organizational commitment to employee retention. Such a process can also monitor and address problems and concerns as they arise. A dynamic induction process can save your organization time and money by producing employees who are more productive sooner. It can also lead to higher employee retention, which means lower turnover, and therefore, lower recruitment costs. The list that follows gives ten good reasons for having a dynamic induction process in your organization; you may find this useful in gaining support for dynamic induction from your own senior management.

Top Ten Reasons for Having a Dynamic Induction Process

1. Create positive first impressions
First impressions are lasting impressions. A positive first impression is the first step to long-term commitment. The first few hours and days on the job create impressions that can take many months, or even years, to change. It is always best for the new employee to see his or her new organization as warm, caring and efficient.

2. Address new-job regrets
Almost any major decision is followed by periods of worry and regret. An effective induction process can help the new employee stop worrying if this was the right job choice and facilitate their feeling good about the decision.

3. Increase comfort levels
Being new on the job brings a certain amount of discomfort. A good induction process will lessen feelings of awkwardness, being lost and out of place and create comfort and confidence in the new employee.

4. Create feelings of belonging
A good induction process can instil feelings of acceptance. New employees will more quickly stop feeling like 'outsiders'. They will become members of the organization, people who are accepted and belong.

5. Make an organizational advocate
With a successful induction process, the new person can speak about the organization with knowledge and pride and therefore become an effective organization advocate.

6. Cut back on trial-and-error learning
All new employees make mistakes, but a good induction process can instil knowledge about organizational policies and procedures and 'how things really work' and can help the new employee make fewer mistakes.

7. Take advantage of the natural enthusiasm of the new employee
Many new employees begin their new jobs eager to get started and do well. Proper induction can channel this natural energy and enthusiasm into productive work and pride in the organization.

8. Shape perceptions and attitudes
Many new employees begin work in their new organization with open minds. To some degree, induction programmes can be indoctrination opportunities. Key values, beliefs, and goals of the organization can be shared and cultivated in the new employee. An understanding of and a commitment to teamwork, quality and total customer satisfaction can begin in an effective induction process.

9. Monitor problems and concerns

As a new employee adapts to the new organization, problems can arise. An ongoing induction process provides opportunities to check for and address the problems and concerns of the new employee.

10. Increase employee connections throughout the organization

Knowing who's who and where to go for what can take some time on the part of new employees. The access to other people, services and information provided by the induction process can help the new employee function more productively and more quickly.

With all of these reasons for having a dynamic induction process, one is often surprised at the number of organizations that have no induction process of any sort, much less a dynamic process. The main reason organizations give for not having induction programmes is that induction is not a high priority. They have more important things to do with their time and effort. The following is a list of common excuses for not giving induction training and my responses to those excuses. You may want to state your own responses in a more diplomatic manner.

Top Ten Excuses for NOT Having an Induction Process

1. We don't have the time for such things. (How much time is being wasted because you don't have a programme?)
2. We can't afford the costs of such programmes. (How much money is wasted on trial-and-error learning, turnover, and recruitment?)
3. Our organization is too small. We don't have enough new employees. (Effective induction can be done on a one-to-one basis.)
4. No one in HR wants to be in charge of it. (It doesn't have to be someone from HR.)
5. The employee handbook takes care of all that stuff. (No, it doesn't.)
6. We've done well enough without it. Why start now? (Ignorance is bliss.)
7. Orienting the new employee is the boss's job. (Is he/she doing it?)
8. Our new employees are very sharp. They don't need induction training. (Think how much smarter they'd be if they had it!)
9. We let the new person watch a load of videos. That works fine. (I see.)
10. There's nothing in an induction programme that can't be learned in a few days on the job. (Or a few weeks, or a few months, or ...)

What Makes an Induction Process Effective?

As the costs of recruiting, training and keeping employees continues to climb, more and more companies have become interested in employee induction but unfortunately there are a number of misconceptions about what is required to make an induction process successful. Try taking the following true-or-false test and see if you have any misconceptions.

Mark the following statements T for true or F for false.

1. For an induction process to be effective, it must be well funded.
2. An effective induction process needs regular care and maintenance.
3. An induction process can be effective without the involvement of management.
4. To be effective, an induction workshop should be led by a professional trainer.
5. A first-rate employee handbook is not essential to an effective induction process.
6. The majority of time in induction workshops should be spent on organizational policy.
7. Employees should attend induction workshops during their first week on the job.
8. Small organizations with few new employees don't need an induction process.
9. An effective induction process begins before the new employee's first day at work.
10. Facilitating employee productivity is the ultimate goal of the induction process.

Now, check your answers with those below.

1. False – While having a well-funded induction process can be very helpful, there is no guarantee that money alone will make the process effective. Dedication, hard work, good planning and effective tools and materials are just as important.
2. True – Things change quickly in today's world. The best programme in the world will soon become outdated, dreary and lacklustre if no one takes responsibility for its upkeep and maintenance.
3. True – Management involvement is not necessary for an induction process to be effective, but the process can be even more effective with management involvement.
4. False – Induction programmes can be effectively led by professional trainers, non-professionals who have been drafted in to do the training, supervisors, managers, HR personnel and any number of other individuals.
5. True – A first-rate employee handbook is nice to have and can be very helpful, but it is not essential to an effective induction programme.
6. False – There is no set rule covering what is the best use of time in an induction workshop. Workshop topics and time allocations

should reflect the goals and objectives of the workshop. What is the best use of the time you have to accomplish your goals?

7. False – Ideally, induction workshops are most effective if attended at some time in the new employee's first month, but that is not always possible. If at all possible, new employees should attend within the first three months.

8. False – All organizations need an induction process. Small organizations with few new employees can still have effective induction. They can utilize one-on-one approaches, as well as online induction materials.

9. True – An effective induction process begins when the new employee accepts the job offer. There are many pre-induction actions that can be taken.

10. True – Employees are recruited to be productive. The induction process should be designed to help facilitate the progress of the new employee towards being as productive as possible.

Your Induction Process

How is your induction process? Does it need fixing? Remodelling? Or does it need a complete overhaul? Take a moment, consider your situation, then take the following assessment and find out!

THE INDUCTION PROCESS ASSESSMENT

Assess each statement below in terms of how descriptive it is regarding the induction process of your organization and circle Yes, No, or Maybe accordingly.

1. Our organization has a dynamic, innovative   Yes   No   Maybe
   induction process, which exerts a real impact
   on the organization by producing employees
   who are more productive sooner.

2. The people in charge of induction in our   Yes   No   Maybe
   organization are enthusiastic about the
   process and do an excellent job.

3. Every new employee is contacted a number   Yes   No   Maybe
   of times prior to their first day on the job
   (by supervisor, colleagues, someone from
   HR, and so on).

4. On an employee's first day, he or she is   Yes   No   Maybe
   met by someone who spends the first hour
   with them, meets them later and takes them
   to lunch, and then gets together with them
   at the end of the day to see how the day went.

5. Our organization considers the new   Yes   No   Maybe
    employee's first week and first month as
    particularly critical times and monitors
    these to enable the new person to become
    a fully productive member of the workforce.

6. Our induction workshop is not a show-and-   Yes   No   Maybe
    tell or a data dump, but a dynamic event
    containing interactive games and activities
    where the participants actually do
    something. Valuable information is
    presented in a variety of interesting and
    informative formats.

7. All the printed material used in our induction   Yes   No   Maybe
    process, including the induction training
    programme, is up-to-date, interesting,
    informative and easy to use. However, we
    do not overwhelm the new employee
    with huge amounts of material and paperwork.

8. New employees leave our induction   Yes   No   Maybe
    workshop feeling good about their job
    choice, informed about the organization
    and enthusiastic about their future.

9. We have an induction website with all   Yes   No   Maybe
    sorts of supporting information available,
    including online induction games and activities.

10. We have a valuable induction companion   Yes   No   Maybe
    programme for all new employees in which
    a work colleague helps guide the new
    person for at least the first few months of the
    new job.

11. Our organization has a number of   Yes   No   Maybe
    employee celebration events beginning with
    celebrating the arrival of the new employee
    and continuing with various celebrations at
    anniversary points and key occasions.

12. New employees in our organization are   Yes   No   Maybe
    part of an ongoing induction process that
    guides and helps them throughout their
    first year of employment.

Now, give yourself two points for every Yes that you circled, one point for every Maybe, and zero points for every No. Add up your total and put your score in the blank below. Check the list that follows for how your programme rates.

Your score: _____

Interpreting your score

20–24 = Excellent! – Congratulations, you have a great programme! Maybe a little renovating here and there could make it even better!

19–15 = Good – a solid programme, but some renovations and repairs might add new energy and make it even better.

14–10 = Fair – renovations may help, but major repairs are what's required.

9–5 = Poor – looks like a major remodelling project is needed. Anything you do will help!

4–0 = Awful! – consider demolishing what little you have and building from the ground up. Anything and everything should help!

IMPROVING YOUR INDUCTION PROCESS

What do you need for your induction process? Review your answers on the induction process assessment above. Consider the interpretation given to your score. Think about your situation and the amount of time, effort and budget you can put into improving your induction process. One of the most essential components of a successful, dynamic induction programme is an individual or a group of individuals who are willing to take responsibility to make their organization's induction process as effective as possible. A few dedicated, hard-working people can renovate, remodel or even construct from the ground up a dynamic, efficient and imaginative induction process. Are you ready and willing to take that responsibility? Are there people who will support you and help you?

Levels of improvement

Consider the four levels of improvement listed below and decide what type of overall improvement project you want to tackle. You may decide upon different levels of improvement for different aspects of your induction process.

Level 1: Renovate –
To give new vigour, to restore to a better condition.
Add new games and activities, improve materials and programmes, energize the whole process.

Level 2: Repair –
To fix something broken or damaged.
Restructure and expand the process, upgrade materials and programmes, add new games and activities, energize the whole process.

Level 3: Remodel –
To alter the structure or style of something.
Redesign and expand the process, change formats, add new components, upgrade materials, add new games and activities, energize the whole process.

Level 4: Build –
To make a structure by putting the parts of it together.
Design and implement a full induction process. Include pre-induction activities; actions for the first hour, day, week and month; a great induction training programme; an induction companion programme and excellent printed and electronic induction materials.

Now that you know what needs to be done, let's look at how you might go about doing it.

Pre-induction Activities

A truly effective and definitely dynamic induction process begins before the new employee's first day of work. It begins when the new employee accepts the job. Pre-induction activities take place between the acceptance of the job and the first day of work. Induction games and structured activities can be used effectively before the new employee's arrival. Such entertaining quizzes, games, and activity sheets can impart important information and create interest and positive feelings in the new employee.

HOW TO INCLUDE THE NEW EMPLOYEE BEFORE THEIR FIRST DAY
The following list gives a number of suitable pre-induction activities:

1. Call the new employee to say, 'Welcome aboard', and see if there are any questions that you can answer.
2. Send the new employee a congratulations gift basket.
3. Send the new employee an information pack containing the organization's newsletters, annual report, brochures, product information and relevant newspaper and magazine articles.
4. Invite the new employee to a company, department or work group social event.
5. Send the new employee tickets to a musical or sporting event.

6. Invite the new employee to have lunch with their new work group a week or two before they begin their new job.
7. See if the new employee would like to have a more complete tour of the organization than they had during their interview sessions.
8. If you are purchasing any new equipment, furniture or supplies for the new person, contact them and get their input!
9. Invite the new employee to come by for coffee. This could also be used as an opportune moment to have their picture taken for their company identification badge.
10. Notify the new person about the organization's orientation workshop or induction programme. Give them the date, time and place that they have been scheduled to attend so that they can get it in their diary.
11. Send the new employee a printed game, quiz or activity sheet with the promise of a prize if they complete it correctly and send it back to you.
12. E-mail the new employee with information about the various games and activities on the company's induction website.

PREPARATION FOR THE NEW EMPLOYEE'S ARRIVAL

There are also a number of actions that can be taken in the workplace prior to a new employee's first day that can facilitate the induction process. Most of these actions revolve around being ready for the new employee. One of the biggest let downs reported by new employees is the feeling that they arrived and no one was expecting them!

The following is a checklist of arrangements that should be made in preparation for a new employee's first day. The more of these arrangements that have been made, the more welcomed the new employee will feel and the more smoothly that first day will run.

- Other workers have received information about the new employee and are aware of the date of the new employee's first day.
- All relevant departments and persons have been notified of the new employee's arrival (benefits, payroll, information systems, accounting, security, reception).
- Someone will be waiting to meet and greet the new employee.
- The new employee's identification badge is ready.
- Everything at the new employee's workplace is ready for use.
- Someone will introduce the new employee to co-workers.
- The new employee's supervisor will spend the first hour showing the new employee around, answering questions and getting tea or coffee with the new employee.
- The new employee has work to do and will be able to keep busy.
- There is an organizational telephone and e-mail directory on the new employee's desk.

- Someone will be taking the new employee to lunch.
- A sign welcoming the new employee has been placed in a central location.
- An induction companion has been assigned to the new employee.
- A small welcoming gift has been placed at the new employee's workplace.
- A printed induction game or activity sheet has been placed on the new employee's desk.
- A welcome-aboard notice with the new employee's name and some basic information about them has been placed on the company induction website.

GAMES FOR PRE-INDUCTION

Games and structured activities can be used as pre-induction activities. The purpose of such games and activities is to share information or to prepare the new employee for the induction training programme. Therefore, some of the pre-induction structured activities might be something for the new person to prepare and bring with them to the training event. If the game or activity is connected to the training programme, the facilitator of the training event would be the person responsible for getting the game or activity materials and instructions to the new person. If the game or activity is informational in nature and part of a number of pre-induction actions, then the responsibility for sending the game and following up with the game will fall to the person handling the pre-induction and early induction activities.

While many of the games and activities presented in Part Two of this book might be adapted for use as pre-induction activities, the following seem most appropriate:

4. Let Me Give You My Card
8. Finding the Words
11. I'm Happy To Be Here, But ...
14. Caption Competition
37. What We Are Famous For
41. TLAs Are Everywhere!

IMPROVEMENT PROJECT FORM
Your Pre-induction Programme

You've looked over ways to include new workers before their first day on the job and you've gone through a list of things that need to happen before a new employee arrives. Now consider your organization's pre-induction programme. What level of improvements need to be made? Do you need to renovate, repair, remodel or build a whole new programme? Mark the appropriate level of improvement below, then fill out your 'to do' list.

_____ Renovate: add a few more activities to include the new worker before the first day.

_____ Repair: add more activities; make more arrangements before the new person arrives.

_____ Remodel: restructure and enhance the entire pre-induction programme.

_____ Build: design and implement a full pre-induction programme.

Your 'to do' list:

_____

_____

_____

_____

_____

_____

_____

_____

_____

_____

The New Employee's Four Firsts

While specific individuals may have different times in the induction process that are particularly important for them, for most new employees there are four critical periods in the induction process. Think of these as the Four Firsts:

- the first hour
- the first day
- the first week
- the first month.

Induction games and structured activities can be used effectively during the new employee's early days on the job. Interesting quizzes, assessments, games and activities can provide important information in an easy and non-threatening way.

Consider your own organization's induction process. Are you doing all that is possible to help the new employee during these four vital periods? The following pages contain things that can be done to help make the new employee's Four Firsts as successful as possible. How does your organization measure up?

The First Hour

The first hour at a new job can be very stressful for new employees. They will often feel a bit nervous and unsure of what to do and, because they want to make a good first impression, they may be hesitant to ask questions. The first hour at the new job therefore presents the perfect opportunity for creating positive impressions and instilling comfort and confidence in the new employee. Having an individual take responsibility for facilitating a new employee's first hour is a critical part of a dynamic induction process. Here are some actions that can be taken to make it a great first hour!

The first hour is critical.

- Commit yourself totally to being with the new employee for their first hour. Don't think about what else you have to do or how quickly you can get this over with. Do it sincerely or don't do it at all.
- Meet the new employee at the main entrance. Don't make them stumble through security procedures alone or try to remember which lift to take.
- Greet the new employee with a warm handshake and a smile. Use the new person's name and be sure you pronounce it correctly.

- Facilitate the identification badge procedure. If possible, have the badge ready and waiting; if not, do what you can to make the procedure as painless as possible.
- Walk with the new person to their office or workplace. Try to make them feel more at ease with a little small talk as you go. Introduce them to people you meet along the way.
- Everything at the new employee's workplace should be ready for use. (This should have been checked out beforehand.) If something of key importance is not ready, apologize and let the new person know when to expect it.
- Walk the new person around the work area. Show them where to hang coats, where the toilets are, where tea and coffee can be had, vending areas and such.
- Introduce the new person to his or her co-workers and to other key people in the workplace. Tell people what the new person will be doing and explain to the new person what the other people do. Do not make judgemental comments about other employees!
- Describe the scheduled activities for the day and, if possible, the week. It is very helpful for the new employee to have some idea of what the first few days will be like.
- Take the new employee for coffee. Show them how to get to the cafeteria or to the break area and tell them about the tea/coffee break routines in the workplace. Explain the rules and common practices regarding eating at your desk, bringing lunch to work, and when and for how long people take breaks and lunch.
- Share the common written and unwritten rules of behaviour. Cover such things as modes of address, dress codes, smoking rules, interpersonal behaviour and start and finish times.
- Go over some of the work that the new person can start immediately. It is very important that people have something to do right away. Let the new person know what to expect for the next few days and weeks in terms of workload.
- Explain any computer and electronic systems. Show the new person the company website, electronic files and how the e-mail system works. Go over what software is available and how to obtain IT supplies and assistance.
- Explain how the telephone system works. Show the new person how to transfer a call, hold a call and how to use the voicemail system. Explain any special rules and regulations regarding long-distance calls, international calls, and conference calls.
- Check the orientation or induction programme. Has the new person been enrolled? When will they be attending? Tell them a little about the programme and what they can expect. If there is an induction companion programme, explain that also.
- Make sure the new employee has lunch plans. Make arrangements in advance for someone to have lunch with the new person. If you

are taking them to lunch, confirm the time with them before you leave.

The First Day

While it is very important to get the new employee's first hour on the job off to a good start, it is just as important that the entire day should be a good one. The first day at the new job creates impressions that last and last and are not easily changed. Just as the first hour needs the sincere commitment of a particular person, the first day goes more smoothly if someone has taken the time and effort to oversee the events of that day. This does not mean that someone must constantly be with the new person, but someone does need to accept the responsibility of monitoring that first day and doing all that is needed to make it a good day.

By the end of the first day, the new employee has:

- been warmly received into his or her new workplace
- met co-workers and key people in the workplace
- toured the immediate work vicinity
- obtained his or her identification badge
- filled out all necessary personnel forms
- settled into his or her workspace
- received all necessary tools, equipment and supplies
- started some type of meaningful work
- met his or her induction companion
- received a schedule of events for the week and month
- obtained a copy of the organization's mission statement, values and so on
- received information on the organizational quality programme
- found a couple of induction games or activity sheets on their desk
- gone to lunch and/or had coffee with supervisor and co-workers
- received names, phone numbers, and e-mail addresses of co-workers
- been shown where the photocopier is and how to use it
- heard about employee service facilities such as an exercise centre, child-care provision, etc.
- received an overview of the work he or she will be doing for the next few days
- met someone at the end of the day to review how the day went.

The First Week

Although the first hour and the first day are perhaps the most critical periods for the new employee, there are still important tasks that need to be carried out during the first week. As the novelty of things begins to wear off, the new employee should feel a little more at ease, but there is still a sense of not quite belonging. It is a good time to make sure that the new person feels included. Below is a list of actions that will enhance that feeling of inclusion.

By the end of the first week, the new employee has:

- been introduced to top management
- met everyone they will be working with
- spent some time with their induction companion
- been notified of when and where to attend induction training
- ordered their business cards
- featured in the company newsletter or intranet, perhaps with an accompanying photograph
- accomplished some meaningful work
- filled out every necessary paper, form and document
- completed and turned in an induction quiz, game or activity
- gone to lunch or had coffee with different co-workers
- received an overview of the organizational and departmental structure
- obtained the organization's mission statement, values and key initiatives
- had one-on-one meetings with all co-workers
- met a supervisor regarding performance standards and expectations
- had an 'end of the first week' review with his or her supervisor.

The First Month

Once the first hour, day and week have gone by, the new employee will usually have met enough people, learned enough about the workplace and have enough work to do that they can keep themselves busy and begin making a contribution. However, this is a time when the new employee may start shaping perceptions and forming attitudes about the job and the organization. A dynamic induction programme should include a monitoring of the first month to make sure that a few key actions, such as the ones listed below, have taken place.

By the end of the first month, the new employee has:

- been introduced to top management
- been introduced at staff and department meetings
- had their picture and profile in the company newsletter
- attended the organization's induction programme
- been meeting regularly with an induction companion
- become productive and is contributing quite satisfactorily
- completed and turned in two or three induction quizzes, games or activities
- received their salary and any due reimbursements

- met their supervisor regarding performance
- attended organizational social events
- become familiar with organizational structure and procedures
- had an 'end of the first month' review with their supervisor.

Games for the Four Firsts

There are a number of games and activities presented in Part Two of this book that can be used in the early days and weeks of the new employee. The following would be most appropriate:

8. Finding the Words
11. I'm Happy To Be Here, But …
12. The New Person in a Group is Like …
13. Reasons I'm Happy To Be Here
14. Caption Competition
20. Treasure Hunt
21. The Best of Everything
22. Where's Where?
24. In Case of Emergency
25. A Sense of Security
28. Money Matters

IMPROVEMENT PROJECT FORM
The Four Firsts in your Induction Programme

As you've gone through the actions to take during a new employee's first hour, day, week and month, I hope you've marked many of them to be included in your dynamic induction process. In fact, as you consider the Four Firsts and your organization's induction process, what level of improvements do you think need to be made? Do you need to renovate, repair, remodel or build a whole new Four Firsts programme? Mark the appropriate level of improvement below, then fill in your 'to do' list.

_____ Renovate: add more activities to the four time periods including the use of games.

_____ Repair: put into practice a number of additional activities for each time period, including the use of games and structured activities.

_____ Remodel: restructure some or all of the Four Firsts; add more activities to each time period and include the use of games.

_____ Build: design and implement a full agenda for each of the Four Firsts including the use of games in each.

Your 'to do' list:

_____

_____

_____

_____

_____

_____

_____

_____

_____

_____

Induction Training Programmes

The length of time spent in an induction training programme and the number of inductees attending such programmes can vary greatly. Induction classes may range in length from a half-day to as much as a week or more and the number of attendees can be as few as six or as many as a hundred plus. The critical factor determining the effectiveness of any training programme, induction or otherwise, is that the quality of its design and delivery must be top notch.

Many of you may be all too familiar with the standard three-hour orientation programme that has too many inductees crowded into a small, hot room with too few chairs and too many long-winded speakers. Endless slide presentations may have given way to endless PowerPoint presentations, but the central goal of getting all that information dumped onto the new employees in the quickest way possible may not have changed at all. The purpose of a truly effective induction training programme is the same as the purpose of an entire induction process and that is to enable the new employee to become a positive, productive member of the organization as quickly as possible.

Many of the goals of the orientation or induction training programme should be the same as the goals of an entire induction process including:

- creating a positive impression
- addressing any new-job regrets
- increasing comfort levels and feelings of belonging
- increasing knowledge of the organization and its policies and procedures
- sharing organizational values, goals and initiatives
- distributing basic staffing and human resource information
- communicating information about the work environment
- sharing job-specific information.

Subjects for the Induction Training Programme

The content of your induction training programme can vary widely depending on what other induction activities you are utilizing in your process. The most common subjects covered in all types of induction materials are found in the following list:

- welcome to new employees
  - new employees introduce themselves
  - reassurance regarding their job choice
  - celebration of their joining the organization

20

- overview of the organization
  - organization's history and current status
  - company size, locations
  - organizational structure
  - organizational vision, mission, goals, etc.
  - company logo, motto, current marketing push
  - company products and services, revenue sources
  - key customers, clients, suppliers and competitors
  - philosophy regarding customers, quality and teamwork
- staffing and HR information
  - benefits and employee services
  - performance standards, rules, policies, procedures
  - company literature: handbook, telephone directory, manuals and so forth
  - safety and security practices
  - legal and compliance issues
  - disciplinary and grievance procedures
  - working hours and overtime, breaks, vacation, sick days, etc.
  - training and education opportunities
- introduction to the work environment
  - local area: road maps, public transportation, local restaurants
  - tour of worksite – toilets, cafeteria, first-aid room, postroom, etc.
  - codes of conduct, dress, smoking, interpersonal behaviour
  - phone use, photocopiers, use of internet and e-mail
  - job content – duties, performance standards
- information on the new job
  - competencies, criteria, performance
  - career paths in the organization
  - the employee's part in the bigger picture

Creating an Effective Induction Training Programme

An effective, dynamic induction process will address all of the subjects listed above through a variety of channels, including printed materials, an induction website, an Employee Handbook, an induction companion programme and an induction training event. The content of your induction training programme will be determined in part by its length as well as the content of the other areas of induction instruction that you are utilizing.

Once you have determined the content of your training programme, you will find the ultimate challenge to be the designing of a dynamic, interesting, involving training programme that combines the welcoming and celebrating of the new employee with the sharing of essential information. The following list gives many of the characteristics of such a programme.

A dynamic induction training programme:

- is well-designed with clear objectives and a smooth flow of events
- has an overall theme that runs throughout the programme and relates to the business
- is held in pleasant, casual surroundings at a convenient location
- provides a good assortment of high-quality refreshments
- has an atmosphere of fun and celebration
- welcomes new employees and puts them at ease
- contains a high level of participation and interaction
- makes use of an assortment of enjoyable, involving games and activities
- uses creative visuals, pleasant sounds and provides things to do
- erases any regrets the employee may have about taking this new job
- addresses the difficulties of being 'new on the job'
- explains what the new employee can expect from the organization
- clarifies what the organization expects from the new employee
- provides important information in a variety of engaging formats
- utilizes only facilitators and speakers with excellent presentation skills
- provides opportunities for new employees to talk, discuss and ask questions
- recognizes the new employees as individuals
- incorporates a reasonable amount of well-designed printed material
- ends with a touch of ceremony as inductees are installed into their new positions.

Energizing Induction Training with Accelerated Learning Techniques

The style and quality of an induction training programme can help to establish a positive impression on new employees and this can be more easily achieved by making use of accelerated learning methods.

Accelerated learning, or brain-friendly learning, is a teaching and learning method based on the latest research. It increases learning effectiveness through the creation of an effective learning environment, the stimulation of all the senses and the total involvement of the learner. The following list suggests ways in which accelerated learning techniques can be used to energize your programme and engage your learners.

1. Create an effective learning environment
   Establish rapport:
   (a) warmly greet participants as they arrive
   (b) give information about yourself
   (c) provide opportunities for participants to interact.

Instil positive expectations:
(a) give a positive purpose and objectives of the course
(b) state optimistic outcomes from participation in the learning
(c) give positive examples and illustrations.
Decorate the learning environment:
(a) have a variety of posters and visual aids on the wall
(b) have a table with literature and product samples
(c) provide an attractive table of refreshments.

2. Stimulate all the senses!
(a) add visual – signs, posters, decorations, handouts on coloured paper
(b) add sound – music, chimes, ring a bell before announcements
(c) add smell – flowers, fresh biscuits or cakes and scented markers
(d) add taste – set out mints, sweets, refreshments
(e) add touch – have samples of products, things to touch and manipulate
(f) use stories, anecdotes, metaphors, and analogies.

3. Use active instead of passive learning techniques
Don't tell, ask – engage the learner with the material to be learned:
(a) use questioning techniques
(b) use lists of questions or problems and let them find the answers.
Involve the participants in the process – give them something to do:
(a) utilize assessments, quizzes, games and activities
(b) use tasks, projects and assignments.
Let them implement what they are learning:
(a) use practice and review activities
(b) have them create their own quizzes and games
(c) let them teach each other about the organization.
Let them learn together:
(a) use small group games and activities
(b) have a variety of partner activities.

Using a Theme

Consider using a theme in the design of your induction training programme. A theme can help create an atmosphere of fun and increase inductee comfort levels. It is also a good way to add cohesion to the programme, to tie things together in a creative and fun way. The following list gives some ideas for themes to stimulate your thinking.

Journey themes lend themselves well to the topic of induction: starting out on a 'new adventure', 'all aboard', 'embarking on a new career', an induction safari and so on.

Sports themes are always popular. If certain sports or particular sports teams are popular in your area, consider a team theme. Use concepts like getting ready for the big game, holding a pre-game warm-up, review of last season and previews of the approaching season.

Detective themes are good for induction training. The new employees are similar to detectives investigating the scene, gathering information and solving the mystery of a new workplace.

Entertainment themes can be fun. Use popular TV shows or films as themes. Do a take-off of a popular game show or talk show.

Business themes reflecting the process or structure of the organization itself are great. If the business is a chain of restaurants with a desert-island theme, hold the induction training 'on a desert island'. If you are in the publishing business, let them put together their own induction books. If you are a medical diagnostic company, let the inductees diagnose their needs as new employees and prescribe their own remedies.

Games for Induction Training Programmes

Certainly induction training programmes are an ideal place to utilize games and structured learning activities. Part Two of this book presents fifty games and activities covering all areas of induction training.

There are games to help people get acquainted, warm-ups and ice breakers, plus games for reassurance and initiation.

Games and activities to get acquainted
 1. Start the Music
 2. Hello, My Name Is …
 3. Induction Round Robin
 4. Let Me Give You My Card
 5. Get Acquainted 4 x 4.

Warm-ups and ice breakers
 6. Three Degrees of Connection
 7. Teacups and Coffee Mugs
 8. Finding the Words
 9. The First Job I Ever Had
10. How I Found This Job.

Reassurance and initiation games
11. I'm Happy To Be Here, But …
12. The New Person in a Group is Like …
13. Reasons I'm Happy To Be Here
14. Caption Competition
15. A Picture Says It All.

There are a wide variety of information-sharing games that cover topics such as understanding the organization, human resources services, legal and compliance issues, and becoming familiar with the new workplace.

General information games
16. Pay Attention
17. A Maze of Information
18. Divide and Conquer.

Games on getting to know the work environment
19. A Walking Tour
20. Treasure Hunt
21. The Best of Everything
22. Where's Where?

Compliance, security and safety information games
23. It's the Law
24. In Case of Emergency
25. A Sense of Security
26. Safety Tips
27. Where's the First-Aid Kit?

Human resources information games
28. Money Matters
29. What's A Person To Do?
30. Overt and Covert
31. What To Do
32. All for You
33. Employee Development Opportunities.

Understanding the organization
34. Once Upon a Time
35. Where in the World is ...?
36. The Big Picture Frame
37. What We Are Famous For
38. Who's Who?
30. Overt and Covert
40. Quality and Customer Service Game
41. TLAs Are Everywhere!
42 Company Quiz Bowl
43. The Company Board Game.

There are also a few games that focus new employees on their new jobs and careers in the organization.

44. Where Do You Fit In?
45. What You Do and How You Do It

46. Measuring Up
47. The Good, the Bad and the Ugly
48. Now, Then and Some Day
49. Putting It All Together
50. Celebration Station.

Not only can these fifty games be looked at in terms of their content, but you may also want to consider them in terms of what they bring to the overall design of your programme. For example, are there points within your training programme where you need to get people out of their chairs and doing something? The following games do just that:

1. Start the Music
2. Hello, My Name Is …
4. Let Me Give You My Card
5. Get Acquainted 4 x 4
10. How I Found This Job
11. I'm Happy To Be Here, But …
13. Reasons I'm Happy To Be Here
19. A Walking Tour
20. Treasure Hunt
21. The Best of Everything
22. Where's Where?
30. Overt and Covert
40. Quality and Customer Service Game
41. TLAs Are Everywhere!

Do you need more activities where the participants get a chance to meet one another and talk with one another for a while? Here are some games and activities to try:

1. Start the Music
2. Hello, My Name Is …
5. Get Acquainted 4 x 4
6. Three Degrees of Connection
11. I'm Happy To Be Here, But …
45. What You Do and How You Do It.

Could you use games and activities that let participants explore the nearby work environment and then return to the training room?

19. A Walking Tour
20. Treasure Hunt
21. The Best of Everything
30. Overt and Covert
40. Quality and Customer Service Game.

Would you like a game or activity that utilizes the artistic abilities of your participants?

4. Let Me Give You My Card
7. Teacups and Coffee Mugs
9. The First Job I Ever Had
15. A Picture Says It All
36. The Big Picture Frame
49. Putting It All Together.

Perhaps you would like an activity that calls upon the acting talents of your participants?

40. Quality and Customer Service Game
45. What You Do and How You Do It
47. The Good, the Bad and the Ugly
49. Putting It All Together.

IMPROVEMENT PROJECT FORM
Your Induction Training Programme

As you've gone through the various subjects for a dynamic induction programme, read about the characteristics of a dynamic induction programme and considered a variety of accelerated learning techniques, I hope you've marked many of them to be included in your induction programme. What type of induction or orientation programme does your organization have? What level of improvements do you feel need to be made? Do you need to renovate, repair, remodel or build a whole new programme? Check the appropriate level of improvement below, then fill in your 'to do' list.

_____Renovate: add new games and activities; utilize more accelerated learning techniques; energize the whole programme.

_____Repair: upgrade materials; add new games and activities; utilize more accelerated learning techniques; energize entire programme.

_____Remodel: redesign the programme; upgrade and revitalize materials; add new games and activities; utilize accelerated learning techniques; energize the whole process.

_____Build: design and implement an entirely new programme; utilize accelerated learning techniques; design top-notch materials; utilize a variety of games and activities.

Your 'to do' list:

_____

_____

_____

_____

_____

_____

_____

_____

_____

_____

_____

Induction Companion Programmes

Companion programmes are a great way to facilitate the new employee's integration into the workplace. Basically, such programmes pair new employees with employees who have been with the organization for a while and are willing to act as a 'go to' person for the new employee's general questions and concerns. The companion can assist the new employee in understanding how things work, where things are and whom to go to for what.

Companion programmes differ significantly from mentoring and coaching programmes. Mentoring programmes are directed at the professional development of a junior employee through the guidance of a more senior employee and coaching programmes are usually intended for specific performance improvement efforts. Again, as with all aspects of the induction process, a good companion programme is focused on producing new employees who are more productive sooner.

Companion programmes can range from being very informal and short term, to very structured and longer lasting. To be most effective, a companion programme requires dedicated individuals who are willing to act as companions and someone to coordinate the programme and take responsibility for making it successful. While a good companion programme cannot replace an entire induction process, it can certainly enhance it. It will also allow induction training programmes to spend more time on organizational history and structure and on basic human resource information and less time on basic 'getting to know the work environment and where things are' and 'doing your job' information.

What Makes a Good Companion?

Ideally, a good companion:

* has been with the organization for at least a year
* is knowledgeable about all aspects of the induction process
* is positive about the organization and the induction process
* does not gossip about co-workers and organizational politics
* enjoys being a companion and helping new employees
* has good interpersonal skills
* contacts the new employee before the first day on the job
* meets the new employee during his or her first day on the job
* is available, within reason, to answer work-related questions
* meets weekly the new employee for the first month or two
* uses games and structured activities as learning tools for sharing information
* keeps the content of discussions with the new employee confidential

- maintains a relationship with the new employee for at least four months.

Games for Companion Programmes

Games and structured activities can be a great help to companion programmes. The coordinator of the companion programme should prepare, and have on hand, a number of games and activities that can be used with companions. If there is in-service training for people who are going to serve as companions, a portion of the training could be devoted to the use of games and structured activities. Games and activities can serve as fun stimuli to begin companion discussions. They can be used as a 'homework tool' between meetings or games and activities can just be a fun way of looking at particular issues and topics in the workplace.

The following is a list of games and activities in Part Two of this book that are particularly useful in companion programmes:

4. Let Me Give You My Card
7. Teacups and Coffee Mugs
8. Finding the Words
11. I'm Happy To Be Here, But ...
12. The New Person in a Group is Like ...
13. Reasons I'm Happy To Be Here
14. Caption Competition
17. A Maze of Information
20. Treasure Hunt
21. The Best of Everything
22. Where's Where?
23. It's the Law
24. In Case of Emergency
25. A Sense of Security
28. Money Matters
29. What's A Person To Do?
30. Overt and Covert
31. What To Do
32. All for You
33. Employee Development Opportunities
35. Where in the World is ...?
36. The Big Picture Frame
37. What We Are Famous For
38. Who's Who?
41. TLAs Are Everywhere!
42. Company Quiz Bowl
43. The Company Board Game
46. Measuring Up
48. Now, Then and Some Day.

IMPROVEMENT PROJECT FORM
Your Induction Companion Programme

Does your organization have an induction companion programme? If so, what is it like? As you read the list of qualities of a good companion programme, did you mark ideas for improving your programme? What level of improvements need to be made? Do you need to renovate, repair, remodel or build a whole new programme? Check the appropriate level of improvement below, then fill in your 'to do' list.

_____Renovate: add more dimensions to the programme; utilize games and activities.

_____Repair: enhance the programme; add more structure; utilize games and activities.

_____Remodel: restructure and enhance the programme; utilize games and activities.

_____Build: design and implement an induction companion programme.

Your 'to do' list:

_____

_____

_____

_____

_____

_____

_____

_____

_____

_____

Induction Instruction Materials

Any printed or electronic materials that have as their purpose the imparting of work-related information to new employees can be considered induction materials. Such materials could include employee handbooks; materials used in induction training programmes; booklets, pamphlets and informational flyers that are put into information packs that are given to new employees; CDs, videos, websites and even e-mail.

The purpose of induction materials is not only to impart work-related information to new employees but also to do so in an effective manner. Therefore such materials should be well designed and easy to use. They should also address induction issues whenever possible, such as creating positive impressions, addressing new-job regrets and creating feelings of belonging.

A simple brochure that contains misspelled words, inaccurate information or that has an arrogant tone can create a very negative impression. On the other hand, an attractive, upbeat brochure that is accurate, informative and easy to understand will create a good impression while it is imparting information to the new employee. It all adds up. Every means of induction instruction is important. Every method can help to assist the new employee to become a positive, productive member of the organization as quickly as possible.

Creating Effective Induction Instruction Materials

What makes induction materials effective? The information must be accurate and easy for the employee to find. The following list presents some simple, useful guidelines for developing printed and electronic materials for induction:

Effective, dynamic induction materials:
- are not big, heavy, bulky or cumbersome
- are easy on the eye with plenty of white space and good design
- have good tables of content and easy-to-use indexes
- have chapter headings that inform and make sense
- use simple, uncomplicated language
- are written and designed in a straightforward, easy-to-follow style
- have well-chosen examples and illustrations
- are continuously updated and improved
- utilize assessments, quizzes, games and structured activities
- are colourful, attractive and appeal to all the senses

Making Use of Websites and Intranets

It is becoming more commonplace to make use of company intranets and websites by creating special sections devoted to induction information. Induction websites can range from simple storehouses of basic employee information to dynamic, highly interactive learning places for new employees. Websites lend themselves very well to the use of games and structured activities. New employees can download copies of quizzes, assessments, game cards and worksheets. They can take a quiz and then e-mail the results to a 'gamemaster' or to their induction companion for scoring. Or alternatively, new employees can take a quiz or play a game and then check for the right answers in another location on the website.

At the very least, an organization's human resources department can put all basic employee information onto a website and include special pages and sections for new employee induction. With a little more effort and ingenuity, a few dynamic games and activities can be added to engage the interest of new employees, and perhaps a few not-so-new employees as well.

Games for Induction Websites

The following is a list of games from the second part of this book that can be adapted for use on induction websites. Some can be adapted easily; others will take more time and effort. Check them out and choose a few for your website.

3. Induction Round Robin
4. Let Me Give You My Card
5. Get Acquainted 4 x 4
6. Three Degrees of Connection
7. Teacups and Coffee Mugs
8. Finding the Words
9. The First Job I Ever Had
10. How I Found This Job
11. I'm Happy To Be Here, But ...
12. The New Person in a Group is Like ...
13. Reasons I'm Happy To Be Here
14. Caption Competition
17. A Maze of Information
20. Treasure Hunt
21. The Best of Everything
22. Where's Where?
23. It's the Law
24. In Case of Emergency
28. Money Matters
29. What's A Person To Do?
42. Company Quiz Bowl

IMPROVEMENT PROJECT FORM
Your Printed and Electronic Induction Materials

How would you describe the printed and electronic induction materials at your organization? Did you mark ideas on the guidelines for developing effective, dynamic printed and electronic induction materials? What level of improvements need to be made? Do you need to renovate, repair, remodel or build a whole new set of printed and electronic materials? Check the appropriate level of improvement below, then fill in your 'to do' list.

_____Renovate: upgrade and streamline materials; utilize games and activities.

_____Repair: upgrade present materials; add new materials; utilize games and activities.

_____Remodel: restructure and enhance the programme; utilize games and activities.

_____Build: design an array of new materials; design and utilize an induction website.

Your 'to do' list:

_____

_____

_____

_____

_____

_____

_____

_____

_____

_____

PART TWO

Dynamic Induction Games and Activities

Contents

Games for Inclusion

Games and Activities to Get Acquainted

1. Start the Music

Overview

PURPOSE

To have participants meet one another quickly and to set an upbeat tone for the training.

SUMMARY

As the facilitator starts playing music, participants get a partner, introduce themselves, and talk for a while. After a minute or two, the facilitator stops the music and participants stop talking, turn, and find another partner. As this continues, the intervals between the music sessions become shorter and shorter.

MATERIALS

Paper and pencils; tape or CD player and lively music; prizes.

TIME

20–30 minutes.

GROUP SIZE

Any size.

Before the game

Set out notepaper and pencils to be used at the end of the game. Look around the room and decide on an area that provides enough room for participants to mix and mingle easily. If you have a large group and there is not much extra space in the room, you might want to consider doing the activity outside, in a hallway, or in any other available space. Have a tape or CD player set up and ready to play music during the game.

Opening lines

How many of you remember playing a game called musical chairs when you were young? This next activity could be called musical partners, because I'm going to use music to help you meet each other in a quick and easy way.

How to play the game

1. Have participants stand in a group in an open area ready to mix and mingle. When the music begins, participants must turn, get a partner, introduce themselves and talk.
2. When they hear the music stop, have them stop talking, turn, and find another partner.
3. This continues for ten minutes, but, as it continues, make the intervals between music sessions shorter and shorter.
4. When the ten minutes are over, call out, 'Time's up,' and have the participants stop and return to their seats.
5. After they return to their seats, distribute paper and pencils and ask them to write down as many names of other participants as they can remember. The participant(s) who remember(s) the most names wins a prize.
6. Conduct a short debrief.

Guidelines for playing

- Energy and enthusiasm from the facilitator helps this activity generate energy and enthusiasm in participants.
- The last two or three rounds should follow one another at ten- or fifteen-second intervals. They should be done very quickly and humorously.

Debriefing

QUESTIONS FOR THE DEBRIEF

1. What happened? How did it feel? What helped?
2. How does this apply to being the new person at work?

POINTS TO BRING FORTH IN THE DEBRIEF

- You're going to be meeting many people in the near future. You want to be able to introduce yourself comfortably and naturally.
- Remember that it will be impossible to remember everyone's name right away.

Variations

- You can make the game more difficult by having participants play the last four or five rounds non-verbally. They can point to nametags and pantomime their jobs, departments, and other information.
- Distribute a handout listing participant names and information and have players check people off their lists as they meet each other. Instead of 'How many names can you remember?' have them try 'How many people checked off on your list can you

© Susan El-Shamy, *Dynamic Induction*, Gower Publishing Limited, 2003

identify?' If people are wearing nametags, of course you will have them remove them prior to this final event!

- You can do this activity without music and simply count aloud, 'one-two-three turn', and have people stop talking and get a new partner.
- Have a theme for the class and use it throughout the training. For this activity, use music related to the theme and have the theme reflected on participant nametags and any other printed materials. Print a listing of participant names and information on brightly coloured paper and display the class motif or theme on the paper in some way.

2. Hello, My Name Is ...

Overview

PURPOSE

To have participants meet one another and to practise introducing themselves to new co-workers.

SUMMARY

Facilitator and participants stand in a circle and take turns going around the circle introducing themselves following a set formula. Prizes are awarded for following the formula.

MATERIALS

Flipchart or notepad; bowl with 100 boiled sweets.

TIME

20 minutes.

GROUP SIZE

8–20.

Before the game

Have two or three bags of individually wrapped boiled sweets (100 sweets or more) and a large bowl or container that will hold 100 pieces set out. Put a flipchart and marker or a large notepad and pencil near the front of the room.

Opening lines

How many of you know each other? Are there people here that you do not know? This next activity will help you meet each other in a quick, easy and fun way.

How to play the game

1. Stand in a circle with the participants. You begin by going around the circle, person by person, shaking hands and introducing yourself, 'Hello, my name is _____ and I work in the _____ department doing _____. I just started this week.' Other participants can respond with, 'Nice to meet you. Welcome aboard.'

2. When you finish, step out of the circle and the person who stood to your left then goes around the circle introducing himself or herself to the group. When they finish, they step out and the next person takes a turn. This continues until only two people are left and they introduce themselves to each other.

3. The group begins with 100 points. You and the participants can keep score on a flipchart or on a notepad. When someone forgets or leaves out any part of the formula, 'Hello, my name is _____ and I work in the _____ department doing _____. I just started this week', the group loses five points. For every point left when the game is over, the group gets a sweet. The sweets can be set out in a bowl for participants to enjoy throughout the day.

4. Conduct a short debrief.

Guidelines for playing

*   Don't rush this activity. The facilitator should model the correct procedure for the group. Stand directly in front of each person you are introducing yourself to, look them in the eye as you introduce yourself, and use a warm, friendly tone of voice. If you haven't made a mistake by the time you are almost finished, you might want to make one just to model how scoring is done.
*   Use individually wrapped boiled sweets for scoring and, at the end of the game, have the group count out the appropriate number of pieces, place them in a bowl, and place the bowl in an appropriate position.
*   Count out the sweets in a dramatic and humorous way.

Debriefing

QUESTIONS FOR THE DEBRIEF

1. What happened? How did it feel? What helped?
2. How does this apply to being the new person at work?

POINTS TO BRING FORTH IN THE DEBRIEF

*   It's important to feel comfortable introducing yourself to your new co-workers.
*   You're going to be meeting many people in the near future and it will be impossible to remember all their names right away.
*   Relaxing, enjoying, and doing the best you can is all you can do.

Variations

*   You can always change the introduction formula to something that better reflects your organization or the focus or theme of your particular induction programme.

- Let the group make up the introduction formula that they feel is best.
- Have some positive, lively music playing in the background to give an upbeat feel to the activity and to keep it moving quickly.

3. Induction Round Robin

Overview

PURPOSE

To introduce the participants to each other.

SUMMARY

The facilitator begins by introducing himself or herself to the group, giving name, where they grew up and went to school, and the position they have. Then the person to the left of the facilitator introduces the facilitator to the group using that information and then gives the same information about himself or herself. The third person introduces the second person to the group using the second person's information and then introduces himself or herself. This continues until the last person is introduced. The facilitator takes notes during the introductions, then quizzes the group and gives prizes for most correct answers.

MATERIALS

Paper and pencils; prizes.

TIME

15–20 minutes.

GROUP SIZE

Up to 12 or so. It may take too long for larger groups.

Before the game

Decide where to conduct this game: in a circle in some part of the room or with participants in their seats and simply turning from one to another. Have paper and pencils set out to use for the quiz. Have a notepad or clipboard ready to take notes and prepare your quiz.

Opening lines

Being new at work always involves introducing and being introduced. For those of you who have already begun your new jobs, this activity will seem quite familiar. For those of you who are just now beginning your new jobs, consider this a practice run for the many introductions awaiting you!

How to play the game

1. You begin by introducing yourself to the group. Give your name, where you grew up and went to school, and the position you now have.
2. The person to your left now introduces you again to the group using the information you just gave and then gives the same information about themselves. Then the person to their left (or in line) introduces that person using the information they just gave and follows by giving the same information about themselves.
3. This procedure is followed until everyone has been introduced.
4. As participants introduce themselves, the facilitator takes notes about the participants.
5. The facilitator distributes pencils and paper, and then gives a quiz based on the information just given by the participants about themselves.
6. Prizes are given for top scores.

Guidelines for playing

*   This game can be played with participants staying in their seats and just turning to introduce neighbours or people in the next row. Or, you may want to ask the two people introducing one another to stand.
*   You can also have participants leave their seats and form a circle in another area of the room.
*   Make the prizes for this game something that can be easily shared, such as small bags of fruit or biscuits.
*   Take good notes as people introduce themselves and each other. Circle or mark information that will make good questions as the game proceeds. When the participants finish, quickly number the circled or marked information in a random order and begin the quiz as soon as possible.
*   Keep it light and fun. Don't make questions too difficult to answer.

Debriefing

QUESTIONS FOR THE DEBRIEF

1. How did it feel to introduce yourself and then have someone else do it?
2. What happened when someone else introduced you?
3. How does this apply to being the new person at work?
4. How easy was it to remember information about each other?

POINTS TO BRING FORTH IN THE DEBRIEF

- People who have just met you and then have to introduce you to someone else may find it difficult to remember everything and will sometimes get things wrong!
- It's not easy to remember lots of information about different people all at once.

Variations

- Instead of where participants grew up and went to school, you could use other information that may be more useful or interesting to the group.
- Have participants write out the information about themselves (name, where they grew up and went to school, and the new position they have) on sheets of coloured paper and hold it up as they introduce themselves and are introduced by someone else. The papers can be posted on the wall after the exercise.
- For a pre-induction activity, post 'card kits' to new employees with instructions for making their special business card. They could be instructed to bring their special business card to their induction training programme.
- As an induction companion activity, the new employee and the companion could both make up cards and bring them to one of their meetings to share and discuss.
- For an electronic version of this activity, e-mail participants a list of class members and ask that they contact one another and gather the information. The first one to e-mail you a complete class list with the correct information on every class participant wins a prize.

4. Let Me Give You My Card

Overview

PURPOSE

To introduce participants to each other in a personalized, creative way.

SUMMARY

Participants write their names and positions on small cards that they also decorate in some meaningful way. They then mix and mingle for a few minutes, introducing themselves to each other using their unique 'business cards'.

MATERIALS

100 3 x 5 note cards; pens and pencils; coloured pencils, crayons, scented markers, stickers; three or more prizes that can be shared.

TIME

30 minutes.

GROUPS

Any size.

Before the game

Have plenty of small cards ready. You will want enough for participants to make four or five cards each. You may want to prepare a table at the back or side of the room to be the production area for the business cards. You can put all of the materials on the table ahead of time. During the activity, send the participants to the production area to make their cards.

Opening lines

How many of you use business cards or are familiar with the use of business cards? Well, this activity we are about to engage in uses business cards, and you can design your own right now!

How to play the game

1. Distribute the 3 x 5 index cards. Have each participant take a few.
2. Tell participants to make themselves business cards with their names, job positions and any other 'fun' information they want to include. Point out the coloured markers and other decorating items at the back of the room. Tell them to decorate their cards in any way they like. Let them know that they have only ten minutes to complete their cards!
3. When they have finished producing their cards, give them ten minutes to mix and mingle, introducing themselves and using the cards.
4. When time is up, ask them to return to their seats. Ask for examples of interesting or clever or funny cards and let participants share and compare for a while.
5. Finally, let the group decide on the funniest card, the most artistic card, and the most unusual card, and award prizes to those three.

Guidelines for playing

*   Keep the activity upbeat and moving fairly quickly.
*   Make your own cards and take part in the activity.

Debriefing

QUESTIONS FOR THE DEBRIEF

1. What happened? How did it feel to make such artistic business cards?
2. How does this apply to being the new person at work?

POINTS TO BRING FORTH IN THE DEBRIEF

*   Sometimes we aren't sure how to act when we are new in a job. We don't know the norms of the new workplace yet.
*   When we are new in a job, we may be concerned about what people will think about us and hesitate to have fun or act silly. We want to make a good first impression.

Variations

*   Instead of a number of business cards, have each participant make one large business card that they hang around their neck or pin to their clothes, then mix and mingle introducing themselves. After the activity, display the business cards on the wall.
*   Add some lively music to the activity, especially when participants are mixing and mingling and sharing their cards.

- For a companion activity, the two people can construct their own large cards before they get together. When they get together, they can exchange cards and discuss them.
- Have inductees electronically design their individual business cards and post them on the induction website. Once all the cards are posted on the website, have participants send you e-mail votes for the best cards. Winners are those ranked among the top three or ten or whatever you decide. Post results on the website in a Hall of Fame so that all players can see how well they did. Send prizes to the winners.

5. Get Acquainted 4 x 4

Overview

PURPOSE

To have participants meet one another and learn a few basic facts about the organization

SUMMARY

Each participant receives a card with 16 boxes, each requiring information. Players mix and mingle signing cards according to the rules. When a player covers either four boxes in a row and four diagonally, or four in a column and four boxes diagonally, he or she comes forward for a prize.

MATERIALS

One Get Acquainted 4 x 4 card for each participant; prizes.

TIME

30–45 minutes.

GROUP SIZE

Twelve or more.

Before the game

Make copies of the 4 x 4 game card on page 56 on thin card. Have plenty of game cards and extra pencils ready. It also works well to have prizes that can be shared.

Opening lines

How many of you have ever played bingo? We're going to play a game now called 'Get Acquainted 4 x 4', and it uses a card similar to a bingo card. But the purpose of this game is to help you meet each other and learn a few facts about the organization.

How to play the game

1. Distribute the Get Acquainted 4 x 4 cards. Explain that each square on the card contains either a description that could apply to someone in the group or a description of an item of information that someone in the group may be able to supply.
2. Explain how to play the game and go over the rules.
3. Distribute pens and pencils to players who need them.
4. Have participants gather in a group somewhere and give them ten minutes to mix and mingle, signing each other's cards, until they win or the time is over. Play some lively music while they mix and mingle and sign cards.
5. When time is up, turn off the music and ask the participants to return to their seats. Announce the winners and have the winners acknowledged by the group.
6. Conduct a short debrief.

Rules for playing

- In order to cover a square, a player must have that square signed by someone in the group who meets that description or by someone who provides the necessary information. For example, if the description says 'The name of the person most recently recruited,' then the participant must find the person in the group who was most recently recruited and have them sign that box.
- A player can have their card signed only once by any individual group member. For example, if I just signed your card for the descriptor, 'The tallest person in the room,' then I can't sign it again in any other box even though I might be eligible for other box descriptors. When people provide information, they should write the information on the card and put their initials next to it.
- Players should ask people directly and specifically about categories. In other words, do not ask, 'Can you sign any of these squares left on my card?' but 'Do you know the year that the organization was founded?'
- Each player may sign another player's card only once. In order to win, a card should have no repeat names (unless there are two or more players with the same name!).
- When any player has four squares signed across and four diagonally, or four down and four diagonally, they take their card to the facilitator who will check for correct answers, no repetition of names, and give out prizes.

Guidelines for playing

- Encourage players to ask directly and specifically about the categories. It's much easier to just call out 'Does anybody work in the Accounting Department?' but it's better for the game if people ask individuals directly, 'Do you work in the Accounting Department?'

Debriefing

QUESTIONS FOR THE DEBRIEF

1. What happened? Which categories did you look for first? Why?
2. Did you make any assumptions about others? How did people perceive you?
3. What did you learn?

POINTS TO BRING FORTH IN THE DEBRIEF:

*   Some characteristics are easy to tell by looking, others are not.
*   Our assumptions are not always true.
*   People do not always perceive us as we think they do.

Variations

*   The ten-minute time limit works best for groups of 12 to 30 people. However, groups vary and sometimes more time is needed. Try giving ten minutes to begin with and adding another five if needed.
*   If you have fewer than 15 people, you may want to allow players to sign other players' cards twice. When people ask if they can sign their own cards, suggest that they try to win using only other people for the first five minutes. Then, if the group has difficulty getting winning cards, you can allow them to sign their own cards.
*   A very large group may need more time to play. For extremely large groups, 60–100 or more, you may want to divide the group into two or three smaller groups for the first five or ten minutes and then let the groups mix for the last five minutes.
*   Construct your own 4 x 4 card content and make it particularly relevant to your organization or group of inductees.
*   If you have an induction website, you could put an Adobe Acrobat file of the 4 x 4 card on the website and players could download and print a copy. Then they could play the game within their department and submit their card to you for a prize.

Get Acquainted 4x4

Have each square below signed by someone in the room who either meets the description or with the correct information which has been provided to you by someone in the room. When you have signed or filled in 4 squares in a row or 4 squares in a column **and** 4 squares diagonally, you win!

Someone who has been with the organization less than a year.	The year the organization was founded.	The person in the room who has been with the organiza-tion the longest.	Someone who works in the accounting department.
Someone who has been with the organiza-tion for more than five years.	The location of the 'head office' or corporate headquarters.	The company or organization logo.	The tallest person in the room.
Someone who works in the same department as you.	A slogan used by the company or organization.	Someone who works in sales.	The name of the Human Resources director.
The person most recently recruited.	The most popular product or service offered by the organization.	The name of the founder of the organization.	The youngest person in the room.

Warm-ups and Ice Breakers

6. Three Degrees of Connection

Overview

PURPOSE

To introduce new employees to one another and have them find common interests and connections.

SUMMARY

Participants are divided into groups of three and given five minutes to find as many ways as possible in which they are all three connected. For example, 'We have a Spanish connection in that Paul studied in Spain, William's sister lives in Spain, and I went on holiday to Spain last summer.' They make a list of their connections and share the list with the whole group. The three participants with the most connections win a prize.

MATERIALS

Pencils and paper; prizes.

TIME

15–20 minutes.

GROUP SIZE

6–24.

Before the game

Set the pencils, paper, and prizes where you can reach them easily. Decide on a place in the room where participants can stand in groups of three and do this activity.

Opening lines

Sometimes when you are new at work, it seems as if you are totally unconnected to the people around you, but it doesn't take long to find interests that you have in common with others. We're going to play a game now in which you will find things that you have in common with each other.

How to play the game

1. Divide participants into groups of three. If necessary, have one group of four, or join with two participants yourself to form a group of three.
2. Give each group a pencil and paper and have them choose someone to be the note-taker for their group.
3. Give the groups five minutes to find as many ways as possible in which they are all three connected, e.g., 'We have a Birmingham connection in that Lucy has a sister in Birmingham, William visited Birmingham last summer, and I went to a wedding in Birmingham five years ago.'
4. When time is up, have the note-taker from each group read out the ways in which that group is connected.
5. Give a prize to the group with the most connections.

Guidelines for playing

*   If people have trouble finding connections, challenge them to look for unusual connections like favourite colour, films they all like, children who support a particular football team, favourite ice creams, television shows, or whatever you choose!

Debriefing

QUESTIONS FOR THE DEBRIEF

1. What happened? Was it easy or difficult to find connections?
2. How does this apply to being the new person at work?

POINTS TO BRING FORTH IN THE DEBRIEF

*   You can't judge by appearances.
*   You have a lot more in common with each other than you might think at first.
*   You have to talk to people to find out what you have in common.

Variations

*   Ask participants to find three job-related connections.
*   Use a larger group of participants, say five or six, and see if they can find three connections.
*   For an electronic version of this game, e-mail participants assigning them into groups of three and ask them to connect electronically. Give a deadline and award a prize to the group with the most connections submitted by that deadline. A period of four to six hours will probably work best unless you have participants from different parts of the world in which twelve or twenty-four hours may be better. Post group connections on your induction website or e-mail them to all participants.

© Susan El-Shamy, *Dynamic Induction*, Gower Publishing Limited, 2003

7. Teacups and Coffee Mugs

Overview

PURPOSE

To have participants introduce themselves and tell something about themselves to the group.

SUMMARY

Participants choose an introductory paper with either a coffee mug or a teacup drawn on it. They put their name and job title on the paper and then decorate the cup or mug in some way that says something about them. Then, one by one, participants introduce themselves and explain the information on their paper to the group.

MATERIALS

Thin card with teacups or coffee mugs printed on them and assorted coloured markers.

TIME

20–30 minutes.

GROUP SIZE

Up to 12 or 15.

Before the game

Make copies of the introductory papers on pages 64 and 65. Make sure that you have enough introductory papers and markers for everyone and set them out where you can get to them easily. Have an introductory paper already drawn up for yourself that you can show as an example.

Opening lines

Any coffee lovers in this group? How about tea drinkers? How many of you like both? In this activity, I'm going to ask you to choose either a coffee mug or a teacup and decorate it in a way that tells us something about you.

How to play the game

1. Distribute introductory papers with teacups and others with coffee mugs and ask participants to take either one or the other.
2. Ask participants to put their name and job title on the paper and to decorate the cup or mug in some way that says something about them. For example, they might choose to write a saying on the cup or mug that describes them in some way, such as 'rather be playing golf,' or they might draw the Eiffel Tower to indicate a trip they have taken recently.
3. Begin the sharing with your own paper, then go around, one by one, having participants introduce themselves and explain the information on their mug or cup to the group.
4. After all introductory papers have been shared, post the papers on the wall of the room and debrief the exercise.

Guidelines for playing

- Adopt a lighthearted attitude for this activity.
- Have some blank paper available for people who do not like coffee or tea. Let them draw their favourite drink!

Debriefing

QUESTIONS FOR THE DEBRIEF

1. What happened? How did you decide what to put on your paper?
2. How does this relate to being the new person at work?

POINTS TO BRING FORTH IN THE DEBRIEF:

- When you are new and you don't know the people around you, you may be hesitant to draw attention to yourself.
- Even a little activity like drinking coffee or tea impacts the workplace. Where is the coffee and tea in your new workplace? Does a trolley come around with coffee and tea? Is there a canteen? Is it all right to drink coffee or tea at your desk?

Variations

- Instead of coffee and tea, use favourite desserts, sandwiches, or biscuits.
- Instead of people explaining their papers, let the other participants guess.
- Have participants decorate a real cup or mug using paint and other materials. Put the cups and mugs on display during the training and have participants take them back to their work sites after the training.

- For a companion activity, have two copies of each paper. Each of you choose one and decorate it to reflect something about yourself. Share and compare papers and use this to lead into a discussion of eating at work. Discuss tea and coffee breaks, eating at your desk, lunch break, where to go for food and drink, and other related topics.
- Have participants submit an electronic cup or mug that is decorated in some way. Post all the cups and mugs on the induction website.

NAME: _____

Position: _____

NAME: _____

Position: _____

8. Finding the Words

Overview

PURPOSE

To define and discuss terms related to induction and orientation and to introduce topics and issues that will be dealt with later in the training.

SUMMARY

Participants are given a word search puzzle and have ten minutes to solve it. The group then discusses the terms on the puzzle. Terms: induction, orientation, inductee, handbook, security, benefits, payslip, compliance, personnel, new, work, job, coffee, tea, lunch, fun.

MATERIALS

One copy of the word search puzzle for each participant; prizes.

TIME

20 minutes.

GROUP SIZE

Any number.

Before the game

Make enough copies of the word search on page 69 so that each participant can have one. You may want to have an overhead transparency of the word search to use for showing the answers.

Opening lines

How many of you do word searches? Could someone explain what word searches are to people who are not familiar with them? I have a short word-search puzzle here that has words in it related to induction and orientation.

How to play the game

1. Distribute a copy of the word-search puzzle to each participant. Remind them that words can run vertically, horizontally, and diagonally and that words can also run forwards or backwards. Tell them they have five minutes to find all the words.
2. Give a prize to anyone who solves it in five minutes. Announce that you will give participants three more minutes and suggest that

© Susan El-Shamy, *Dynamic Induction*, Gower Publishing Limited, 2003

participants work together to see if they can find all the words in the time left.

3. When the three minutes are up, give prizes to all who have completed the puzzle. Have them share the answers with each other.

4. Go through the words in the puzzle, giving definitions and discussing what the terms mean. Let participants know when and if the terms/topics will be covered later in the programme.

5. Have a short debrief.

Guidelines for playing

- If some people are not familiar with word searches, show examples.
- If there are many participants who have not done word searches before, you might want to have the group work together in pairs right from the beginning.
- Use the words in this game as an introduction and overview to the rest of the induction programme. For example, when you go over the answers and get to words like 'salary, benefits, and pension,' you can mention if and when those topics will be covered in the programme. You can give quick information about topics that are not covered later in the programme, as you go through the answers. For example, where do people eat lunch? Where do you get tea and coffee?

Debriefing

QUESTIONS FOR THE DEBRIEF

1. What happened? What was easy? What was difficult?
2. How does this apply to being the new person at work?

POINTS TO BRING FORTH IN THE DEBRIEF

- When we are accustomed to doing or seeing something one way, it is difficult at first to see it or do it in another way.
- It's easy to overlook simple things.

Variations

- You can make a copy of the puzzle on an overhead transparency and have the group do the puzzle together giving you instructions to mark the words.
- Let small groups create their own word searches then share them with other groups and try to solve each other's puzzles.
- For a companion activity, have two copies of the word search ready and each of you try to find the words. Whoever gets done first can

help the other. Then use the words on the puzzle to guide a discussion of the various issues: induction, orientation, inductee, handbook, security, benefits, payslip, compliance, personnel, new, work, job, coffee, tea, lunch, fun.

- Send out an Adobe Acrobat file (a PDF) of the puzzle and have participants download it. The first person to solve the puzzle and get it back to you electronically gets a prize. They can print it out, solve it, and fax it to you. Or they can make a copy of the PDF, solve the puzzle, then make a PDF of the solution and e-mail it back to you.

I	N	D	U	C	T	I	O	N	C
K	P	I	L	S	Y	A	P	O	Y
N	F	S	Y	P	S	G	M	H	T
O	E	T	T	N	A	P	G	A	I
I	E	I	E	O	L	E	N	N	R
T	F	F	F	I	A	R	I	D	U
A	F	E	A	S	R	S	K	B	C
T	O	N	S	N	Y	O	R	O	E
N	C	E	A	E	T	N	A	O	S
E	Z	B	W	P	X	N	P	K	Q
I	N	D	U	C	T	E	E	J	W
R	B	H	C	N	U	L	O	E	D
O	W	O	R	K	C	B	N	U	F

INDUCTION	SALARY	SAFETY	PARKING	WORK
ORIENTATION	BENEFITS	SECURITY	LUNCH	JOB
INDUCTEE	PENSION	COMPLIANCE	COFFEE	NEW
PERSONNEL	PAYSLIP	HANDBOOK	TEA	FUN

9. The First Job I Ever Had

Overview

PURPOSE

To get people talking about work and the workplace and sharing what they are looking forward to in this job.

SUMMARY

Participants get paper and coloured markers and have a few minutes to draw a picture of the first job they ever had. They then share their experiences and talk about the benefits of employment and what they are looking forward to in this job.

MATERIALS

Paper and coloured markers.

TIME

20–30 minutes.

GROUP SIZE

Up to ten or twelve.

Before the game

Have a pile of thin card or flipchart paper ready to distribute. Have coloured markers set out on the tables or ready in small containers to be passed around. It is also helpful if you have a sample picture already drawn of your first job that you can share with the class.

Opening lines

How many of you remember the first job you ever had, the first time you were paid for doing some type of work? This next activity will make use of some of those memories.

How to play the game

1. Distribute paper and coloured markers and give participants a few minutes to draw a picture of the first job they ever had.

2. One by one, have participants show the group their picture and talk about the first job they ever had. Encourage them to share what they are looking forward to in this job.
3. After each participant shares and talks, make comments and get the group to discuss some of the features they are looking forward to in their new jobs.
4. Have participants post their papers on the wall or hang them from the tables in front of their name cards.
5. Conduct a short debrief.

Debriefing

QUESTIONS FOR THE DEBRIEF

1. How did it feel to remember and discuss your first jobs?
2. What have you learned about yourself and the world of work from past jobs that you can now use in this new job?

POINTS TO BRING FORTH IN THE DEBRIEF

*   New jobs bring new opportunities to learn and grow.

Variations

*   Instead of drawing pictures, you could just have participants verbally share information about the first job they ever had. They could first share with a partner and then the facilitator could ask for interesting examples.
*   Instead of the first job, you could have participants talk about the best job they ever had and what made it such a good job.
*   Instead of individual pictures, have the group do a wall mural illustrating all of their first jobs. Give them a time limit, say fifteen minutes, and let them decide how to go about doing it.
*   Divide the class into three or four small groups and let each group choose a first job from among its group members and do a pantomime of that job. See if the other groups can guess the jobs.
*   Have a bulletin board on the induction website and ask each participant to post a short paragraph about their first jobs, then have them read the various paragraphs and vote for the funniest, the most unusual, and so forth.

10. How I Found This Job

Overview

PURPOSE

To show common approaches to finding jobs and lead into discussion of co-worker concerns about how people get their jobs.

SUMMARY

Participants mark a checklist to indicate how they found and obtained their job. They then share and compare their lists (school interview, answered advertisement, referred by friend or family member, employment agency, website information) and sign one another's lists for methods that they have used. The first person to find someone in class who has used each of the methods listed and has them sign his or her paper wins a prize.

MATERIALS

Checklists; pens and pencils; prizes.

TIME

20 minutes.

GROUP SIZE

Any size.

Before the game

Have a checklist ready for each participant. Set the checklists, pens, and pencils out where you can reach them easily. Make a copy of the checklist on page 75 for each person attending. Decide on an area of the room where participants can mix and mingle easily.

Opening lines

How many of you did a fair amount of job hunting before you found this job? Has anyone ever asked you at some time how you found that job? Well, as a way to get you acquainted with each other and to find out how people find jobs, I've got a short activity for you.

How to play the game

1. Distribute checklists for finding jobs to the participants. Ask them to take a moment or two and mark off any item on the list that they used in their most recent job hunt.
2. Give participants ten minutes to mix and mingle and talk with one another, sharing and comparing how they found this new job they have. When they find a participant who has used one of the items listed, they should ask that person to sign on their list next to the item they used.
3. Give a prize to the first person to find someone in class for each of the methods listed.
4. Conduct a short debrief.

Guidelines for playing

- Once all participants have the list and have gone through it and marked off methods that they have used, quicken the pace of the game by stating: 'You have five minutes in which to find people in the group who have used these various methods and to have them sign your sheet. I'll let you know when there is only one minute left!'
- If there is a small group, you may want to join in the activity yourself to add more possibilities for winning!

Debriefing

QUESTIONS FOR THE DEBRIEF

1. What happened? Which methods were easy to find? Which were difficult?
2. How does this apply to being the new person at work?

POINTS TO BRING FORTH IN THE DEBRIEF

- There are always concerns among workers about how people found their jobs, or, perhaps more accurately, how people got their jobs.
- Finding and getting a job often includes both planned and unplanned methods.

Variations

- With large groups of people, do this activity in small groups of four to six people. Have individual participants mark their papers first, then put people into groups to share and compare. The group that has used the most methods gets a prize.

- Make a large wall poster of 'Ways to Find a Job' and have the participants list different ways with drawings and illustrations. Participants can then sign their names under ways that they have used and write comments regarding those ways.
- The wall poster idea above could be done electronically on a bulletin board or through e-mails.

How I Found This Job

_____ school job listings, school interview

_____ newspaper advertisement

_____ advertisement in a journal

_____ advertisement in association newsletter

_____ heard about it from a friend or family member

_____ heard about it from the friend of a friend

_____ stopped by the main office and inquired

_____ telephoned inquiry to the organization

_____ information on organization's website

_____ employment agency

_____ internet job search

_____ wrote a letter of inquiry

_____ other:

_____ other:

Reassurance and Initiation Games

11. I'm Happy To Be Here, But ...

Overview

PURPOSE

To acknowledge the mixed feelings involved in starting a new job.

SUMMARY

A one-page handout covered with positive, negative, and neutral adjectives is distributed and participants are asked to circle two positive and one negative adjectives that describe how they are feeling. They then circulate and attempt to find someone else in the group who has circled the same three adjectives.

MATERIALS

Handouts for all participants.

TIME

20–30 minutes.

GROUP SIZE

Any size.

Before the game

Make copies of the checklist on page 81. Have a checklist ready for each class member. Set the checklists, pens and pencils out where you can reach them easily.

Opening lines

How many of you are experiencing mixed feelings about starting a new job? That's the way it is for most of us when we start any new experience. This next activity lets you explore those mixed feelings.

How to play the game

1. Distribute the handouts and ask participants to circle two positive words and one negative word that describe how they are feeling about their new job.
2. Give participants five minutes to circulate, sharing and comparing the words they have circled.

3. Tell them that when they find another participant who has exactly the same three words circled as they do, they should come to you for a prize.
4. When participants come to you with the same three words circled, give them each a small prize and put a check mark on their papers. They can then continue to share and compare with other participants.
5. When the five minutes are up, call time out and have everyone return to their seats. Do a short debrief.

Guidelines for playing

- Keep the activity quick and simple.
- If you have a very large group, you might want to give them ten minutes.

Debriefing

QUESTIONS FOR THE DEBRIEF

1. What happened? How did it feel? Which words were circled most often?
2. What was the purpose of doing this activity? What did you learn?

POINTS TO BRING FORTH IN THE DEBRIEF

- Most people begin a new job with mixed feelings.
- Many people starting new jobs have similar feelings.

Variations

- Divide participants into small groups and let them come up with their own words. Have each group choose the four words they most want to use. Combine all the words from all the groups into a master list of words. Have each participant write the master list on a piece of paper and circle the three that most apply to them.
- Have participants construct a wall poster of adjectives with drawings and illustrations.
- For a companion activity, use this handout to stimulate a discussion of the mixed feelings that come with starting a new job.
- Let participants build an adjective list on the induction website and then have each choose three adjectives and share and compare the results.

I'm happy to be here, but …

GLAD   *Nervous*   Excited

CONTENT   **HAPPY**   Worried

anxious   *tense*   CURIOUS

Eager   SATISFIED   **Ready**

ECSTATIC   inquisitive

overjoyed

EDGY   ELATED   PREPARED

calm   cool   **THRILLED**

apprehensive   DELIGHTED

nosy   *stressed*

Interested   Pleased

12. The New Person in a Group is Like ...

Overview

PURPOSE

To open a discussion of the difficulties of being the new person in a group.

SUMMARY

A one-page handout covered with pictures of various objects is distributed. In small groups, participants generate ways to complete the phrase, 'Being the new person in the group is like ..., because ...' using an item from the handout and clever sentence completions. The groups then share their results.

MATERIALS

Handouts for all participants; prizes that can be shared.

TIME

20–30 minutes.

GROUP SIZE

6–24 participants.

Before the game

Make copies of the handout on page 84. Set the handouts, pens, and pencils out where you can reach them easily.

Opening lines

Being the new person at work can be awkward at times and it is often difficult to describe to someone else. This next activity lets you attempt to describe how it feels.

How to play the game

1. Divide the participants into small groups of three or four and give each group a handout.
2. Give the groups five minutes to choose objects from the handout

and devise descriptions of what it is like being the new person in a group using the objects in the phrase, 'Being the new person in a group is like _____ because _____.'

3. Have each group do as many as they can in five minutes. Ask them to choose their best description.
4. Have a large, blank flipchart posted on the wall and when groups have chosen their best analogies, have them write them on the chart.
5. Let the whole group decide on the funniest, the craziest, and the most accurate descriptions and give those groups a prize.
6. Conduct a short debrief.

Guidelines for playing

• Keep this activity lively and funny.
• If participants want to come up with their own analogies, that's great.

Debriefing

QUESTIONS FOR THE DEBRIEF

1. What happened? How did it feel to have to come up with analogies?
2. Why did we do this activity? What did you learn?

POINTS TO BRING FORTH IN THE DEBRIEF

• There are common awkward feelings that people have when they are the new person in a group.
• Talking and laughing about the awkwardness is helpful.

Variations

• Have the group brainstorm analogies for objects that you hold up, project on a screen, or hold up pictures of.
• Have the group construct a wall poster of analogies complete with illustrations and decorations. Conduct the debrief with all of you standing at the poster.
• Let small groups of participants come up with their own analogies and present them to the whole group. Have the presentations done non-verbally with participants acting out or pantomiming the analogies.
• Use the handout to stimulate analogies with your partner in the companion programme and then let it lead into a discussion of being new on the job and what that is like.
• Post pictures on the induction website and for a set period of time, have participants list their analogies under the pictures. After the time limit, have participants vote on the best analogies.

The New Person
in a Group
is Like ...

because

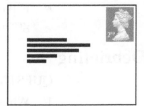

  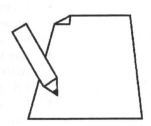

13. Reasons I'm Happy To Be Here

Overview

PURPOSE

To reassure and validate job choice and to let new employees know that the organization is happy to have them.

SUMMARY

Each participant gets a handout listing reasons to be happy working for the new organization and checks off three reasons that describe them. Participants then share and compare their choices. The activity ends with you sharing a list of reasons why the organization is happy to have the new employees.

MATERIALS

Handouts for all participants.

TIME

20–30 minutes.

GROUP SIZE

Any size.

Before the game

Make copies of the handout on pages 87 and 88. Set the handouts, pens, and pencils out where you can reach them easily.

Opening lines

After you've been in a new job for a while, people ask you questions like, 'How's it going?' and 'Are you happy with your new job?' This next activity will give you practice in answering those questions.

How to play the game

1. Give participants a copy of the handout and ask them to check off at least three reasons why they are happy with their new jobs.

2. Have participants stand and mix and mingle for five minutes sharing and comparing the reasons that they have checked.
3. Debrief the sharing and comparing activity, then end by sharing the list of reasons the organization is happy to have these new employees. The list can be transferred to an overhead, simply read aloud to the group or copies can be made for all.

Guidelines for playing

- Keep the pace quick and upbeat. When you get to the reasons the company is happy to have them, read them off dramatically or reveal them one at a time with a dramatic effect.

Debriefing

QUESTIONS FOR THE DEBRIEF

1. What happened? Which items were most popular?
2. How does this apply to being the new person at work?

POINTS TO BRING FORTH IN THE DEBRIEF

- New jobs usually start very positively.
- There are benefits to both the organization and the employee.

Variations

- Reveal the reasons one at a time on a screen.
- Let small groups of participants make up Top Ten lists of their own and then share them with the group.
- Have the list of reasons posted on the induction website and ask participants to respond to the list.
- For a companion activity, have a copy of both handouts. Begin with the reasons 'I'm happy to be here' and let the new person check off two or three reasons. Discuss those reasons, then look through the reasons the organization is happy to have the new person.
- Ask individual participants or small groups of participants to come up with lists of reasons they are happy to be in their new jobs and post them on the website. E-mail them your own list of why the company is happy to have them and also post that list on the website.

Reasons I'm Happy To Be Here

It beats being unemployed.

It's a good place to be until my acting career takes off.

It's the kind of job that I've always wanted.

I'm working with some really great people.

I live nearby so I'll save money on commuting.

I have a nifty desk with a comfortable chair.

The work is challenging and enjoyable.

It's interesting working with such weird characters.

It's much better than the last job I had.

I will enjoy being part of such a respected organization.

It feels great to be out of school and making some money.

I really like my job title.

This job will let me apply my creativity.

The people I'm working with are very nice.

I think I can learn and grow as a person in this job.

This job will give me a chance to build my skills.

There are a lot of attractive people working here.

It's nice to get a payslip.

This job gives me a sense of identity and purpose.

I have a wide variety of things to do so I'll never be bored.

This job is just one important step in my incredible career.

Reasons the Organization Is Happy to Have You

It's better than having nobody in that position.

We can say we knew you before your acting career took off.

You're the kind of employee that we've always wanted.

You become one more really great person working here.

Since you live nearby you'll always be on time.

That nifty desk and comfortable chair will now be used.

We know you'll enjoy the challenging work.

You'll fit right in with all the weird characters.

You're better than the last person who had that job.

You will help make this a respected organization.

We want you to feel great and make some money.

Everyone really likes your job title.

We want you to apply your creativity.

The people you're working with are very nice, so you'll fit in.

We want you to learn and grow as a person in this job.

We want you to build your skills in this job.

A lot of attractive people here will be watching you.

It's nice to give a good worker their payslip.

This job will give you a sense of identity and purpose.

With a wide variety of things to do, you'll never be bored.

This job is just one important step in your incredible career.

14. Caption Competition

Overview

PURPOSE

To get the group laughing and talking about what it feels like to be new on the job.

SUMMARY

Participants are given flyers with cartoons drawn on them depicting different new employee situations and told to come up with captions for the cartoons.

MATERIALS

Handouts; pens and pencils; prizes.

TIME

30 minutes.

GROUP SIZE

Any size.

Before the game

Make copies of the handout on page 89. Set the handouts, pens, and pencils out where you can reach them easily.

Opening lines

How many of you have heard stories of funny mistakes that new employees have made? How many of you have ever made a funny mistake at work? How many of you plan to make a few in your new job? This next activity deals with such situations.

How to play the game

1. Divide the participants into small groups of three or four and give each group a copy of the handout.
2. Tell the participants they have ten minutes to come up with as many funny captions as possible.
3. When the time is up, show the cartoons one by one on an overhead projector and have the different groups share their captions. Let the group choose their favourite caption for each cartoon.

4. Give a prize to the group with the most chosen captions and a few special prizes for funniest caption, most realistic caption, and so forth.

Guidelines for playing

- Groups do not have to have a caption for each cartoon. Let them decide which cartoons they want to offer a caption for.
- As you play this game with various classes, keep some of the funniest captions and share them at the end of this activity. Maybe you can choose one caption from each class for the Caption Hall of Fame.

Debriefing

QUESTIONS FOR THE DEBRIEF

1. What happened? Which cartoons were most difficult? Which were easiest?
2. How does it feel when you make a funny mistake at work?
3. What is the best way to handle such situations?

POINTS TO BRING FORTH IN THE DEBRIEF

- Mistakes are bound to happen when you are new on the job.

Variations

- For a quicker variation of this activity, hang large copies of the cartoons along the wall and have participants write captions under them. As a group, walk around, read the captions and choose the funniest.
- Use some quiz show sounding music as participants work on their captions.
- Give groups a number of cartoons, but let them decide on only three or four that they generate captions for.
- For a companion activity, each of you take a copy of the handout and try to come up with captions. Share what you come up with and then work together to do a few more. Use this to stimulate a discussion on the difficulties of being new on the job.
- Post the cartoons on the induction website and let participants offer captions. Have them give their names with their captions and all the participants can then vote on the funniest, the best, the most accurate, and so forth. Have a Hall of Fame for the cartoon captions voted best.

15. A Picture Says It All

Overview

PURPOSE

To highlight issues around what it is like to be 'new'.

SUMMARY

Small groups of participants are given coloured markers and large sheets of paper and have ten minutes to draw a picture illustrating what it's like to be the 'new person at work'.

MATERIALS

Large sheets of paper; coloured markers; prizes.

TIME

30 minutes.

GROUP SIZE

Any size.

Before the game

Make sure you have plenty of paper and coloured markers. Decide where this activity will take place. If the participants are seated at tables, they can do the activity at their tables; otherwise, you may want to tape the papers to the wall and have small groups gather around the papers.

Opening lines

Is there anyone in the group who is creative or artistic? Good, your fellow classmates may find you very valuable in this next activity.

How to play the game

1. Divide the participants into small groups of four to six people and give each group a large sheet of paper and some coloured markers.
2. Tell them they have ten minutes to draw a picture illustrating what it's like to be the new person at work. Encourage them to be creative and have fun with this.

3. When the time is up, have each group present their drawing to the rest of the class and discuss/debrief relevant points as they come up.
4. Let the group decide on which drawings receive prizes for funniest, most creative, and least artistic talent displayed.

Guidelines for playing

- Keep it light and fast moving.
- If the drawing is done at tables, wait until after each group presents their drawing and you facilitate discussion of the drawing, then post it on the wall. Keep them posted during the training.

Debriefing

QUESTIONS FOR THE DEBRIEF

1. What happened? What was difficult? What was easy?
2. How did you decide what to do?
3. What common themes do you see in these drawings?
4. How does all of this relate to being new on the job?

POINTS TO BRING FORTH IN THE DEBRIEF

- Beginning a new job brings a mixture of feelings.
- Tasks that are difficult can be less difficult when done in a group.

Variations

- Do this activity as a mural. Have a large, long section of white paper taped to the wall and have the groups assigned to different areas along the wall.
- Give general directions to the group and let them decide how they want to carry out the task; individually, small groups, or as one group.
- Instead of just paper and coloured markers, provide a variety of art supplies including such items as coloured paper, scissors, tape, buttons, pieces of cloth, glitter, paste, stickers, labels, and magazines from which they can cut out pictures to use.
- Have some invigorating music going on in the background as participants create their artwork.
- Have a bulletin board or mural available on the induction website and ask participants to contribute their own artwork illustrating what it is like to be the new person at work.

Games for Sharing Information

General Information Games

16. Pay Attention

Overview

PURPOSE

This question and answer matching game is used to keep people attentive and involved during an induction training session.

SUMMARY

At the beginning of the programme, participants receive a list of questions and possible answers. Then throughout the training session, you and various speakers provide information that can be used to match the questions with the right answers.

MATERIALS

Question and answer sheets; pencils; a grand prize and other prizes.

TIME

Varies according to the length of the programme.

GROUP SIZE

Any size.

Before the game

Construct a simple fill-in-the-blank questionnaire using questions related to the content of the training. Put in questions from all of the major content areas. If there are guest speakers, check with them ahead of time and put in questions that they will be providing answers to in their presentations. Try to have the very last question or two cover content that comes in the last segment of the training. When you have the quiz the way that you want it, make enough copies for everyone.

To add extra motivation for this game, make the grand prize something special that will have particular value for the participants. For the other prizes, you might want something with the company name or logo such as pens, hats, t-shirts, cups, or whatever you like.

Opening lines

How many of you are good at taking quizzes? How about fill-in-the-blank quizzes? That's the type of quiz I'm going to give you right now! And you've got all day to find the answers!

How to play the game

1. Distribute the quiz and ask participants to look over the questions quickly.
2. Explain that throughout the induction programme, participants will be given information that answers the various questions. If they pay attention, by the end they should have gathered enough information to answer all of the questions correctly.
3. Announce that the first person to answer all of the questions correctly will win the grand prize and that anyone else who answers all of the questions correctly before time is up (set a time limit near the end of the programme) will also win a prize.
4. Explain that information might come from you and various materials that you will be using, and may also come from visiting guest speakers.
5. When time is up, congratulate all winners and go over the correct answers.
6. Conduct a short debrief.

Guidelines for playing

- It is important that the answers come up naturally in the programme material and not look as if they have been deliberately stuck into the material. It is also a nice touch to have guest speakers deliver some of the answers. You may also want to have the answers to one or two of the questions in the materials that you distribute during the programme.

Debriefing

QUESTIONS FOR THE DEBRIEF

1. Which questions were the most difficult to answer?
2. What information will be the most useful to you?
3. Why did we play this game?

POINTS TO BRING FORTH IN THE DEBRIEF

- Information comes from a variety of resources.

Variations

- Play the game with partners or small groups of three or four participants working together to find the right answers.

© Susan El-Shamy, *Dynamic Induction*, Gower Publishing Limited, 2003

17. A Maze of Information

Overview

PURPOSE

To present any basic information (general, financial, policy, and so forth).

SUMMARY

Small groups of participants receive blank crossword puzzle sheets and lists of questions regarding the topic being addressed. Their task is to find the answers to the questions and then create a crossword puzzle from those answers. Each small group receives a different list of questions. The first group to finish receives a prize. Their final puzzles are put onto large flipchart pages. When all the groups are finished, they post their puzzles on the wall and the group reviews all the puzzles and the questions and answers.

MATERIALS

Blank crossword puzzle sheets; large grid-style flipchart sheets; lists of relevant questions; materials that can provide the answers to the questions; prizes.

TIME

45–60 minutes.

GROUP SIZE

6–18.

Before the game

Decide on the type of material that you want to cover in this activity. You may want to have each group work on a different sub-topic within one basic topic. For example, a topic like basic company information could have sub-topics like company history, company organization, company products and services, and so on. On the other hand, you might choose to have each group work on completely different topics such as finance, security, human resources, training, and so forth. Use your own time limits and induction goals to help you decide how much to include.

To keep the activity relatively short, use small groups of three or four participants and make each list of questions only eight to ten items long. Have information (pamphlets, brochures, handbooks, online access, and so on) spread out on a side table where participants can easily get to it.

Speed this activity along by having a sample list of questions and a crossword puzzle ready to use as an example.

Sample items

Across
1.   Company administering the pension plan: _____ International
2.   Payslips are sent out on the first _____ of the month.
3.   This department handles all pension and insurance matters.
4.   This department issues parking permits.

Down
1.   The _____ office makes all international travel arrangements.
2.   The time at which the cafeteria opens in the morning.
3.   Official organizational appraisals are given _____ times a year.
4.   Your employee ID badge must be renewed every _____ months.

Opening lines

Is there anyone in the group who likes to do crossword puzzles? I'll have to make sure that you are all in separate groups for this next activity so that your classmates can all benefit from your individual skills.

How to play the game

1.   Divide participants into small groups of three or four people.
2.   Show the participants a sample of questions and a crossword puzzle and answer any questions participants have regarding the process.
3.   Give each group a list of questions regarding the chosen topic(s), a few blank crossword puzzle sheets, and one large grid-style flip-chart page. Point out the information available in the room.
4.   Tell the groups to find the answers to the questions and then create a crossword puzzle from those answers. Encourage them to be creative in the design of their puzzle.
5.   Explain that they will have 20 minutes to find the answers to their questions and to construct their puzzles. Their final puzzle should be put on the large flipchart page and posted on the wall. Explain that the first group finished will receive a prize.
6.   Give a prize to the first group to finish. When all the groups are finished and have posted their puzzles on the wall, have each group present their puzzle and go through the questions and answers with the group. At the end of each puzzle review, distribute any information related to the content of the puzzle.
7.   Conduct a quick debrief and give prizes for the prettiest puzzle, the ugliest puzzle, the funniest puzzle, and so forth.

Guidelines for playing

- Keep the puzzles short and simple. The focus should be on the information and not on the intricacies of puzzle design!

Debriefing

QUESTIONS FOR THE DEBRIEF

1. What happened? What was easy and what was difficult?
2. Did you acquire any helpful information?

POINTS TO BRING FORTH IN THE DEBRIEF

- You never know what information will be needed in the future.

Variations

- The facilitator can collect the puzzles and send them out to class members at a later date or use them in future classes.
- If you can spare the extra time it takes, make copies of the various puzzles and have each group solve all the other puzzles in order to win.
- Do a companion version of this game. The companion can give the new employee the blank puzzle sheets and a time limit in which to prepare a puzzle. Then the two of them can get together and see if the companion can solve the puzzle successfully.
- For an e-version of this game, the blank puzzle sheet could be made into a PDF and sent to new employees who could then print it out and make up their own puzzles. They could fax or e-mail their puzzle to the facilitator. If more than one new employee is playing, each could receive an e-mail copy of the game directions, a blank puzzle sheet, a list of questions, and a list of other people playing the game. They could send their finished puzzles to each other until they have all completed all of the puzzles.

18. Divide and Conquer

Overview

PURPOSE

To facilitate participants finding the answers to key questions that they have on four chosen topics.

SUMMARY

Participants generate key questions on four chosen topics and are then divided into four groups. Each group is assigned a topic and the questions for that topic. Using employee handbooks and various other forms of information, participants quickly find the answers to the questions.

MATERIALS

A variety of information on four chosen topics; stopwatch; prizes.

TIME

30 minutes.

GROUP SIZE

8–24.

Before the game

Decide on the topics you want covered in this activity. It works well with subjects like work hours, time off, insurance, and pay deductions. Gather a variety of information on each of the topics, including employee handbooks, and have it nearby to distribute to the group.

Opening lines

How many of you received a packet of information from the HR department after you accepted your new job? There's a lot of information involved when you join a new organization isn't there? We're going to take a little time now to divide up some of that information and see if we can conquer it!

How to play the game

1. Explain that there are four topics of information that they will be dealing with in this activity and write the four topics on a flipchart leaving a little space after each one.

2. Ask the whole group to generate a few key questions for each topic. For example, if the topic was working hours, questions might include: 'What holidays do we get off?' or 'How many sick days do we get each year?' Write down their questions as they come up. After you've generated questions on all topics, have the group vote on the five key questions they most want answered under each topic. Circle the five chosen questions under each topic.

3. Divide the participants into four groups and distribute the information among the groups. Tell them not to open the hand-books or any information until you say so. Tell them they have five minutes to find the answers to the questions for their topic. Any group that has found their five answers in five minutes wins a prize.

4. Hold up the stopwatch and have them pause a few seconds while you wait for the second hand to get to twelve. When it does, say, 'Go!'

5. After exactly five minutes, yell, 'Stop'. See how many groups have found all of their answers and distribute prizes.

6. Review their questions and answers. Let participants look up answers to any remaining questions and conduct a short debrief.

Guidelines for playing

• Make the activity even shorter and assign each group three questions and allow only three minutes.

Debriefing

QUESTIONS FOR THE DEBRIEF

1. What happened?
2. What did you learn?
3. Why did I have you do this activity quickly?

POINTS TO BRING FORTH IN THE DEBRIEF

• The information is out there. It's just a matter of taking the time to find it.

Games on Getting to Know the Work Environment

19. A Walking Tour

Overview

PURPOSE

To acquaint participants with new co-workers and with their new work environments.

SUMMARY

Co-workers from the workplace pair up with new employees and take them on a 20-minute tour of major sites around the workplace.

MATERIALS

Maps and a list of sites for a walking tour; a number of co-workers from the work site who can make themselves available for this activity; a variety of prizes and thank-you items.

TIME

30–45 minutes.

GROUP SIZE

Works best with small groups where new employees take tours one-on-one with other employees, or, at most, with only two or three inductees per regular employee.

Before the game

Put together a list of the major points of interest at the worksite. Include places like the cafeteria, employee lounge, exercise facilities, coffee kitchen, vending machines, supply closet, smoking areas, and mail-room. Your tour should also include items like unusual artwork, company awards, portrait of the CEO, and so forth.

Before the training begins, leave an appropriate number of stickers at each point of interest. For example, in the employee lounge, you might leave a small container filled with stickers and marked, 'Induction participants' on a table. As participants visit each point of interest, they should pick up a sticker and place it on their list of sites. Place a few unique or unusual stickers among the offerings and at the end of the game give prizes to the individuals or groups who have those stickers.

You will also have to find a few current employees who can come to the training for an hour and participate in this activity. Ideally, try to get people who are friendly, positive, and will treat this assignment as a pleasure, not a painful task. Be sure to make their experience a rewarding one in some way.

Opening lines

How many of you have ever taken a tour of a city, a neighbourhood, a famous building? Well, for the next half hour or so, you will be taking a tour of this building! And here to serve as your tour guides are a few fellow employees I'd like you to meet.

How to play the game

1. Introduce the visiting employees from the worksite to the participants.
2. If there are enough visitors, pair each new employee with a visitor; otherwise, divide the participants into small groups and assign one visitor to each group.
3. Distribute maps and lists of sites for the walking tour. Ask everyone to look over their lists and ask if there are any locations that need clarifying.
4. Assign pairs or small groups to begin at different locations and then proceed in order according to their lists. If you have only a few groups, assign them to locations that are two or three apart on the list. This will avoid lots of people showing up at the same time at the same location.
5. Explain that this is not a race, but a walking tour. It is also an opportunity to meet new people and an opportunity to ask questions and gain information from a fellow employee who has been here a while.
6. Tell participants to be sure to pick up a sticker at each site so that they have proof that they have been to each site!
7. When everyone has returned, do a quick debrief, and end the activity with awarding prizes to those individuals and groups who have the prize stickers.
8. Finally, end with a group 'thank you' to the visitors.

Guidelines for playing

- If possible, conduct this activity before a break period and invite the visitors to stay during the break and have refreshments.
- Try using small coloured circle stickers in a variety of colours with just a few of a certain colour mixed in. Or if you use a variety of other stickers, again, put just one of a certain colour or style in each location.

- Try to arrange the order of sites visited in such a way as to cause the least amount of disruption possible to the rest of the workplace.

Debriefing

QUESTIONS FOR THE DEBRIEF

1. What happened? How did it feel to take a tour of your workplace?
2. What did you learn?
3. Any other comments, questions, concerns?

POINTS TO BRING FORTH IN THE DEBRIEF

- After we get settled in our jobs, we often don't see areas of the workplace that we are not connected with in some way.
- Co-workers who will help when you need it are extremely valuable.

Variations

- Have the participants and the visitors create their own list of the places they would like to see and put together the walking map and itinerary in such a way that there is a good flow of traffic.

20. Treasure Hunt

Overview

PURPOSE

To acquaint participants with their work sites.

SUMMARY

Participants are divided into small groups of three to five and given lists of objects and information to collect from various locations throughout the workplace. All team members must collect the objects and information on the list at the same time. All teams that return with all the items on the list win a prize.

MATERIALS

Lists of items to be found; prizes.

TIME

45 minutes.

GROUP SIZE

Up to 30.

Before the game

Decide on eight to twelve locations that you want participants to visit and what items they can bring from the various places. For example, they can pick up employee handbooks at the Human Resources office, get brochures from the employee exercise facility, get a copy of this week's lunch menus from the cafeteria, and so forth. Be sure to check with each site ahead of time to warn them and make sure they have enough of the items that will be sought after. In addition to the eight to twelve sites on the list, you may want to add two or three additional items for each group to obtain such as a photograph of the founder, a product of the company, a coffee mug with the company logo, a pencil with the company name on it, and so on. Prepare two or three versions of the treasure hunt list with the items in different order. Hopefully, this will lessen the chance of everyone showing up at the same place at the same time. Make enough copies for each team.

Opening lines

How many of you have ever been on a treasure hunt? In this next activity you will each be collecting a treasure of information and maybe a gold medallion or two!

How to play the game

1. Divide the participants into teams of three to five people. Let each group choose a team leader and give that leader a pirate hat to wear.
2. Give each team a treasure hunt list and tell them they have twenty minutes to gather all of the items and return to the room. Explain that the gathering of items must be done as a team. That is, they must all go together to the various places and whenever possible, they should each obtain a copy of the item.
3. Give a prize to each team that returns with all of the items on their list before the time is up.
4. When everyone returns, distribute the prizes and debrief the activity.

Guidelines for playing

*   Don't make the additional items on the list too difficult to find. The point of the game is to work together, see the workplace, and gather information.

Debriefing

QUESTIONS FOR THE DEBRIEF

1. What happened? How did it feel to go on a treasure hunt at work?
2. How did the team leaders feel about wearing the pirate hat?
3. Why do you think I asked you to play this game?
4. What did you learn?

POINTS TO BRING FORTH IN THE DEBRIEF

*   Information is everywhere, but it is not always easy to find.

Variations

*   Use a pirate theme throughout the game. Give everyone a pirate hat to wear. Prizes can be chocolate 'gold medallions' or small treasure chests of treats.
*   For a companion activity, the companion can give the new person a treasure hunt list and allow twenty minutes for them to gather all the items. The two can then go over the items and discuss different aspects of the organization related to the items.

- Post a list of treasure hunt items for people to find before the training begins and ask them to bring the items to the training. Add a new item each day for a week or so before the programme and make the last addition thirty minutes before the programme begins. Give a prize to each participant who shows up with all the items!

21. The Best of Everything

Overview

PURPOSE

To introduce inductees to other employees in the workplace and to gather information about where to find the best products and services in the area.

SUMMARY

Participants go on an information hunt in their new workplace and gather opinions from other employees regarding where to find the best tea, coffee, breakfast food, vending machines, sandwich shops, Indian restaurant, place to get some peace and quiet, conference room, and so on.

MATERIALS

Lists of items to get information about; prizes.

TIME

45 minutes.

GROUP SIZE

Any size.

Before the game

Put together a handout entitled 'The Best of Everything'. Along the left-hand side list such items as tea, coffee, breakfast foods, vending machines, sandwich shop, fish and chips, nearby pub, Chinese take-away, Indian restaurant, place to get peace and quiet, conference room, and any other items you feel are appropriate or pertinent to your workplace. Leave enough room at the bottom of the handout for inductees to add a few items of their own. Make enough copies of the handout and have it nearby for this activity.

Opening lines

Does anyone know of a good Indian restaurant nearby? How about a good place in this neighbourhood to get fish and chips? It always takes time to find the best places, doesn't it? Well, this next activity may help speed up finding 'The Best of Everything'.

How to play the game

1. Give each participant a copy of the handout and explain that these are items that new employees often like to find out about. Solicit additional items from the group and have them add the new items to the list.
2. Divide the participants into small teams of three to six people. Explain that their task is to interview at least four people each and gather information about 'The Best of Everything' listed on their handout. They should do this individually for fifteen minutes, then gather into their groups and compile their data.
3. Ask that participants use good judgement and try not to interrupt employees who are busy working. Suggest that they interview employees in the cafeteria, the hallway, at the coffee stations, and so on. Tell them to introduce themselves to the employees they interview and explain that they are in the new employee training programme.
4. Say that they have fifteen minutes to gather data, then they should meet in their groups for another ten minutes and be ready to report their findings at a given time.
5. When time is up, have the groups report their findings while you list their findings on a flipchart. When all the data is in, have the class produce a final flipchart of 'The Best of Everything' and post it in the room.
6. Give a prize to the group with the closest match of items on their final list with the final list of the class.
7. Do a quick debrief.

Guidelines for playing

- To quicken the pace of this activity, have each group choose a group leader and use the group leader to help keep the group on task.

Debriefing

QUESTIONS FOR THE DEBRIEF

1. What happened? How did it feel to question people you don't know?
2. What did you learn?
3. How will you use what you learned?

POINTS TO BRING FORTH IN THE DEBRIEF

- Your fellow employees can be a great source of information.

Variations

- As a companion activity, give the new employee the list at the end of one session and ask for it to be filled in by the next time you get together. At the next session, you can discuss the findings.

22. Where's Where?

Overview

PURPOSE

To help new employees learn where things are located and where to go to get certain things done.

SUMMARY

Using a large map of the area, participants are asked to find bus stops, trains and subways, eating places, and shopping places nearby. Then a large map of the company or organizational grounds is posted and participants locate various groups and divisions in the organization. Finally, a map of the building and the different floors is used to help participants locate various departments and offices, the cafeteria, and other relevant areas.

MATERIALS

Large wall maps of the area, the grounds of the organization, and the main building; different coloured wall chart pins or small round coloured stickers; prizes.

TIME

30 minutes.

GROUP SIZE

Six to twenty or so.

Before the game

Find good, colourful maps of the area, the company grounds, and the main building. Have these enlarged and posted on the wall of the training room. Put together three lists: one containing areal items of interest such as bus stops, train stations, local eating and shopping establishments, and so on; a second listing various buildings, organizational divisions and groups, and important organization landmarks; and a third list with various departments and offices, the cafeteria, the daycare centre, the health and fitness centre and other relevant areas in the building. Make the three lists contain the same number of items. There should be at least ten or fifteen items on each list, twenty if possible.

Gather local and company pamphlets, brochures, handouts, maps, and other materials that give information related to the three lists and have it available on a nearby table.

Opening lines

Did anyone get lost trying to find this training room today? Has anyone become lost trying to find other offices or departments in the organization? This next activity should be helpful in learning what is where!

How to play the game

1. Point out the three large maps on the wall and ask if anyone has had a chance to look at the maps. Divide the participants into three groups and assign each group to one of the maps.
2. Ask the participants to stand and go over to the maps. Give them a minute to look over all three maps and then have the groups go to their assigned map.
3. Give each group a set of pins or stickers and each person in the group a list of the places they are to find. Point out the information on the table that they can access. Tell them they have fifteen minutes to find their items and mark them on the map. (Give less time if there are fewer items.)
4. Give a prize to the first group to find all of their locations and correctly mark them.
5. When all groups are finished, ask a representative from each group to show the rest of the participants their map and the places they have marked. Give each participant a copy of all the maps and all the lists.
6. Conduct a short debrief.

Guidelines for playing

• If the groups have five or more people, use a group leader to keep the groups focused and on task.
• Make the maps the best quality possible. A little extra time and effort to find and reproduce good maps makes a big difference to the success of this activity.

Debriefing

QUESTIONS FOR THE DEBRIEF

1. What happened? What was easy to find? What was difficult?
2. What did you learn from this activity?
3. How will you use what you learned?

POINTS TO BRING FORTH IN THE DEBRIEF

- Having a sense of where things are helps you feel more at ease in a new environment.

Variations

- If you have the time, let the groups generate their own lists of what they want to know about and then find where things are.
- This makes a good companion activity. You can put the maps up on a wall or lay them out on a table. Work together to find the items on the lists.

Compliance, Safety and Security Games

23. It's the Law

Overview

PURPOSE

To present basic compliance issues and health and safety information.

SUMMARY

Participants take a true-false quiz covering various legal and compliance issues related to employment, health and safety, and so on.

MATERIALS

True-or-false quizzes; a few prizes that can be easily shared.

TIME

30 to 45 minutes.

GROUP SIZE

Any size.

Before the game

Gather the general information that is usually distributed to new employees regarding employment legal issues, health and safety legal issues, and other compliance information. Go through the information and mark what you consider to be the ten or twelve most important facts that you would like new employees to know. Next, construct a true-or-false quiz covering those ten or twelve facts. Design the items for the quiz in a straightforward manner, but don't make them too easy. It is always fun to find facts that sound as if they could be false, but in reality are true. Include a few items that give information about why a law is important or what happens if compliance is not followed.

Have copies of the quiz ready and waiting.

Opening lines

How many of you like to take true-or-false quizzes? Would you rather take such a quiz by yourself or with a partner? Well, I have a true-or-false quiz for you to take and I'll let you decide whether you want to take it alone or with a partner!

How to play the game

1. Distribute the quiz and let people take it alone or with a partner. Give them ten minutes to complete the quiz.
2. When time is up, create a courtroom atmosphere. Put on a wig. Pull out a gavel and bang it a couple of times as you announce, 'Time is up!'
3. Go through the quiz, item by item, discussing the issues and the answers. Use the gavel to announce true or false as you give the answers to each item; afterwards read the actual law.
4. Distribute any related handouts, brochures, or materials as you go through the quiz.
5. Give prizes to those with top scores and conduct a short debrief.

Guidelines for playing:

- Do this activity quickly and in an upbeat manner, however, when important or serious issues are being discussed, be sure to treat them seriously.

Debriefing

QUESTIONS FOR THE DEBRIEF

1. What happened? Which items were most difficult? Why?
2. Why is it important to the organization that you know about these issues?
3. Why did I get dramatic with this activity and use the wig and gavel?

POINTS TO BRING FORTH IN THE DEBRIEF

- Some procedures and requirements may seem annoying or unimportant, but they can be very important to the organization and have damaging ramifications if not followed.

Variations

- For a companion activity, take the quiz together and discuss the various items. You can then look through information that the organization has on health and safety and various compliance issues.
- Put this quiz online. Have the sound of a gavel rap loudly after every entry of an answer and then present the law behind the answer.

24. In Case of Emergency

Overview

PURPOSE

To acquaint participants with basic information on what to do in emergency situations at work.

SUMMARY

Participants take a multiple-choice quiz regarding what to do in a variety of emergency situations. Information covers facts like emergency exits, emergency procedures, first-aid location, fire extinguishers, and so on.

MATERIALS

One quiz for each participant; prizes.

TIME

20 minutes.

GROUP SIZE

Any size.

Before the game

Go through the information that your organization has for employees regarding what to do in an emergency situation. Construct a multiple-choice quiz with eight to ten questions covering the most important information. When designing the multiple choices, use variations of the pattern that follows:
(a) a plausible answer, but not the right answer
(b) a funny answer, but not altogether unreasonable
(c) the right answer
(d) a ridiculous answer
(e) a combination of answers a and b; or a and c; or all of the above.

Opening lines

How many of you remember taking tests at school? Did you ever have a teacher tell you 'Keep your eyes on your own paper. No cheating!'? I have a short test for you to take right now, but let's try something. If you get to a question and you don't know the answer, I'd like you to look over at your neighbour's paper and see what they have put down. Borrow their answers if you like. OK?

How to play the game

1. Distribute the quizzes and tell participants that they have ten minutes to answer all of the questions.
2. After a few minutes, ask if they are having difficulty with any of the questions. Encourage people to look at each other's papers and help one another with the answers.
3. When everyone is finished, go through the items one by one and discuss the answers.
4. Give small prizes to everyone who got a perfect score.

Guidelines for playing

• Do this activity quickly but add a very quick review at the end. Ask people to set aside their tests and answer the questions as you ask them one last time!

Debriefing

QUESTIONS FOR THE DEBRIEF

1. Why did we do this activity?
2. What kind of emergencies do you feel least prepared for?
3. How can you be better prepared?

POINTS TO BRING FORTH IN THE DEBRIEF

• Discussing possible emergencies and how to handle them helps us be prepared should they arise.

Variations

• For a companion activity, each of you take the quiz and then share and compare your answers.
• Put the quiz online!

25. A Sense of Security

Overview

PURPOSE

To acquaint participants with general information regarding organizational security issues.

SUMMARY

Participants take a true-or-false quiz covering a variety of security issues and then review and discuss the correct answers.

MATERIALS

True-or-false quizzes; prizes.

TIME

20–30 minutes.

GROUP SIZE

Any size.

Before the game

Gather the general information that is usually distributed to new employees regarding security issues. Go through the information and mark what you consider to be the ten or twelve most important facts that you would like new employees to become aware of. Next, construct a true-or-false quiz covering those ten or twelve facts. Design the items for the quiz in a straightforward manner, but don't make them too easy. It is always fun to find a fact or two that sound as if they could be false, but in reality are true. Mix the true and false questions and do not have more than sixty per cent of either kind.

Here are a few examples:

1. All persons in the building must wear company
    badges at all times.   True/False
2. Personal computers being carried in and out of the
    building must be registered at the front desk.   True/False
3. A record is kept of all documents copied on
    company copying machines.   True/False

4. There are security cameras mounted in all
   hallways, common rooms, and public areas.   True/False

Prepare a handout with the correct answers and additional information for each question. Have the quiz and the handouts set out where you can reach them easily.

Opening lines

How many of you were asked to show your identification badges at the front desk this morning? That's just one of many security measures that the organization uses. We're going to discuss a number of other security issues now.

How to play the game

1. Ask people to get a partner and distribute the quiz. Give them ten minutes to complete the quiz.
2. When most participants are finished with the quiz, ask the partners to turn and form groups of four. Ask the groups of four to compare and discuss their answers.
3. Go through the quiz, item by item, discussing the issues and the answers. Distribute any related handouts, brochures, or materials as you go through the quiz.
4. Give prizes to those with top scores and conduct a short debrief.

Debriefing

QUESTIONS FOR THE DEBRIEF

1. What happened? Which items were most difficult? Why?
2. Why is it important to the organization that you know about these issues?

POINTS TO BRING FORTH IN THE DEBRIEF

• Security procedures and requirements may seem bothersome or unimportant, but they can be very important to the organization.

Variations

• For a companion activity, have the new person take the true-or-false quiz covering a variety of security issues and then review and discuss the correct answers.

26. Safety Tips

Overview

PURPOSE

To acquaint participants with basic safety issues in the workplace.

SUMMARY

Participants brainstorm safety issues and concerns that they think are pertinent to their workplace and then check in company materials to see how many they guessed right and if they missed any.

MATERIALS

Employee handbooks or organizational materials concerning safety issues.

TIME

20–30 minutes.

GROUP SIZE

Any size.

Before the game

Gather information on safety issues and concerns for your workplace. Have copies of the information available for each participant.

Opening lines

Have any of you ever had an accident or been hurt at work?

How to play the game

1. Divide participants into small groups and tell them they have five minutes to brainstorm as many safety issues and concerns as they can think of for their workplace.
2. After five minutes, have the groups stop their brainstorming and share the items. As they give various issues and concerns, discuss these issues and concerns and list them on a flipchart.
3. When all their issues and concerns have been listed, distribute safety materials and ask participants to look through the materials quickly and see if all their issues and concerns are covered.

4.   For anything that is not covered in the materials, tell them that you will send that information to the people who put together the safety materials and hopefully it will be included in the next printing!

Debriefing

QUESTIONS FOR THE DEBRIEF

1.   Why did I ask you to generate your own list of safety issues?
2.   What did you learn by doing so?
3.   Why is the company so concerned about safety?

POINTS TO BRING FORTH IN THE DEBRIEF

•   Issues of safety in the workplace are a very real concern to us all.

27. Where's the First-Aid Kit?

Overview

PURPOSE

To raise participant awareness of how to handle simple accidents in the workplace.

SUMMARY

In small groups, participants discuss health and safety situations in the workplace and how they should deal with them.

MATERIALS

Handouts.

TIME

30 minutes.

GROUP SIZE

Any size.

Before the game

Put together a handout of eight or ten common emergency medical situations that occur in the workplace. Include situations like the following:

- someone faints and falls to the floor
- someone hits their head on an open file drawer
- a swarm of wasps comes through an open window
- someone runs a staple through their finger
- someone has a heart attack
- someone spills burning hot tea on your leg.

Add examples of real incidents from your own workplace. Get examples from people in the HR department or the first-aid office if you have one. Talk with colleagues and check in the employee handbook to see what should be done in each situation.

Opening lines

If someone, right now in this class, accidentally cut their hand and began to bleed profusely, what should we do?

How to play the game

1. Divide the participants into small groups and distribute the list of situations.
2. Tell them they have ten minutes to discuss the situations and decide on what should be done.
3. When the ten minutes are up, go through the situations one by one, discussing what actions should be taken. Make sure that by the end of the discussion, new employees know where the first-aid room is, if you have one, and where the first-aid kits are kept.

Guidelines for playing

- Keep this activity short and directed at the most common situations and solutions.
- You may want to include one or two funny emergencies such as a large mouse running through the office or a few bats hanging from the rafters.

Debriefing

QUESTIONS FOR THE DEBRIEF

1. Which situations seemed most likely to occur?
2. How do you typically respond in emergency situations?
3. Why did I ask you to do this activity?

POINTS TO BRING FORTH IN THE DEBRIEF

- Accidents happen in the workplace and it pays to be prepared.

Variations

This activity can lead into a good companion discussion. The companion could also walk the new person to the first-aid office, then show them where the first-aid kit is kept and so forth.

Human Resources Information Games

28. Money Matters

Overview

PURPOSE

To acquaint new employees with the typical deductions that are taken from their pay and with other related money matters.

SUMMARY

Participants are given sample payslips and must guess the percentage of pay that is taken out in each of the deduction categories.

MATERIALS

A large copy of a typical payslip with the various deductions highlighted to post on a wall; copies of the same payslip to distribute; a general handout on payslips, deductions, and related matters; prizes.

TIME

20–30 minutes.

GROUP SIZE

Any size.

Before the game

Get a copy of a typical payslip and gather information on the amount taken out for various deductions. Check with accounting and other departments concerned and make sure your information is accurate. Put together a general handout on payslips and typical deductions. As far as possible, give information not only about where the money goes, but also what it is used for.

Construct a sample payslip with the various deductions listed, but leave out the amounts. Make copies of the sample payslip for all participants.

Construct an extra large sample payslip that can be posted on the wall for this activity.

Opening lines

How many of you can remember a time when you were waiting for your first payslip? You had worked out how much you were going to receive and you were already planning on how to spend it, and then what happened? You received the payslip and a surprise! It was less than you expected! Why?

How to play the game

1. Distribute the sample payslips. Explain that the various deductions are listed but point out the blanks where amounts are missing.
2. Ask participants to fill in the blanks with their estimates of the percentage of their pay that will be withheld for each deduction category.
3. Have participants share their estimates with a partner and see how they compare. Now have the partners pair up into groups of four and again share and compare. Ask each group to decide on deduction percentages for each category.
4. List the deduction categories on a flipchart and ask each group for their estimates.
5. Distribute the handout on payslips and typical deductions. Post the large payslip on the wall. Go through the information on the handout and have participants check their estimates with the information they now have.
6. Award prizes to the group that most closely matched the real amounts.
7. Conduct a short debrief.

Guidelines for playing

- As you go through the various deductions, give information about where the money goes and what happens with it.

Debriefing

QUESTIONS FOR THE DEBRIEF

1. What happened? Did people overestimate or underestimate?
2. What did you learn?
3. Why did we do this?

POINTS TO BRING FORTH IN THE DEBRIEF

- There is always less money than we hoped there would be.
- Money that is deducted goes somewhere and serves a purpose.

Variations

- For a companion activity, each of you take the quiz and guess the amounts of the various deductions, then check the answer sheet and see how you did. Use this activity to lead into a discussion of pay and benefits.
- Put this activity on the induction website.

29. What's A Person To Do?

Overview

PURPOSE

To acquaint participants with disciplinary and grievance procedures.

SUMMARY

In small groups, participants go through a list of situations and options that are listed for the people in the situations and then choose what they think are the best options. You then read the situations providing information on disciplinary and grievance procedures and together the group decides on best options.

MATERIALS

Handouts listing situations and options; materials and handouts on organizational grievance and disciplinary procedures; prizes.

TIME

30–45 minutes.

GROUP SIZE

Any size.

Before the game

Gather information on your organization's disciplinary and grievance procedures. Go through the material and pull out a few basic definitions and information regarding the steps to be taken in disciplinary and grievance procedures. Produce a one- or two-page handout to be used in this exercise.

Get copies of organizational brochures, pamphlets, or handbooks regarding disciplinary and grievance procedures. Make sure you have enough for all participants.

Prepare a handout listing half a dozen situations in which someone might file a grievance or in which a manager or supervisor might take disciplinary action. Choose fairly standard situations. The idea is to raise awareness of personal rights and standard procedures, not to exchange lurid possibilities or outrageous past situations. Let people from the human resources office look over the situations and your handouts to check for accuracy and to make any comments and suggestions that will help you in this exercise!

Set the handouts where you can get to them easily during the training programme.

Opening lines

Our next topic is nobody's favourite topic, but just in case you ever need the information, let's spend a little time talking about disciplinary and grievance procedures.

How to play the game

1. Distribute the handout with basic definitions and information regarding the steps to be taken in disciplinary and grievance procedures. Go through the material briefly and then say that it helps to better understand the material if there are example situations.
2. Hand out the example situations and then divide the participants into small groups of three to six people. Tell them they have ten minutes to go through the situations and decide what they think the person in each situation should do.
3. When the ten minutes are up, ask each group to make their final decisions and circle the best option for each situation.
4. Go through the situations and lead a short discussion on each. See if the large group can reach consensus about the best option for each situation. When all situations have been discussed and the group has decided what each person should do, check to see which small group has the most options matching the final chosen options of the large group and give them a prize.
5. Conduct a short debrief of the activity.

Guidelines for playing

- Keep this activity quick and fast moving. The purpose of this activity is to share information about disciplinary and grievance procedures, not to get into deep, involved workplace personality conflicts. If you see the discussion moving into inappropriate territories, say so and get it back on track, fast!

Debriefing

QUESTIONS FOR THE DEBRIEF

1. What happened? Why were some of these situations difficult to discuss?
2. What was the purpose of this activity?
3. What did you learn? Why do organizations have such set procedures for taking disciplinary action and filing grievances?

POINTS TO BRING FORTH IN THE DEBRIEF

- Hopefully, you will never encounter disciplinary and grievance procedures, but just in case, it's good to have some basic information.

Variations

- For a companion activity, go through the list of situations and the various options that are listed for the people in the situations and discuss what the two of you think are the best options. Then go through copies of organizational brochures, pamphlets, or handbooks regarding disciplinary and grievance procedures.
- Put a version of this game on the website and let participants generate their own situations and responses.

© Susan El-Shamy, *Dynamic Induction*, Gower Publishing Limited, 2003

30. Overt and Covert

Overview

PURPOSE

To explore the written and unwritten rules of conduct.

SUMMARY

Participants review the written rules of conduct for their workplace, then generate and discuss the possible unwritten rules. Finally, participants do a bit of reconnaissance in the workplace to gather information about unwritten rules.

MATERIALS

Handouts or handbooks with material on rules of conduct.

TIME

45 minutes.

GROUP SIZE

6–20 participants.

Before the game

Go through your organization's handbook or other material that describes general rules of conduct and guidelines for employee behaviour. Become acquainted with company stated policy. Have enough copies of such material ready for all participants.

Do some investigation of your organization's unwritten rules. Visit different departments and talk with people. See what the unwritten rules of conduct and getting ahead are. Do people go home on time or stay late? Do they have neat and tidy desks, or messy desks indicating they have too much work to do? Is having food at the desk frowned upon, or do people eat lunch at their desks?

Opening lines

How many of you are familiar with the terms overt and covert? Overt is that which is done openly and explicitly and covert is that which is done secretly and not talked about. This next activity looks at some overt and covert organizational behaviours.

How to play the game

1. Distribute the material on rules of conduct and employee behaviour. Go through the material with the participants, and then begin a discussion on some of the unwritten rules of behaviour in the workplace.
2. Begin a list of unwritten rules on a flipchart. Use examples like official work hours vs. staying late; clean desk vs. messy desk; business casual vs. business formal; and so forth.
3. Ask for examples of differences in dress and behaviour codes among functions (sales, design, service, technology, and so on) and departments.
4. Tell participants that they will now go on a ten-minute reconnaissance mission into the workplace to gather information about unwritten rules. They must each go into the workplace and observe behaviour. If possible, they should go to their new departments and talk to one or two people.
5. Tell them to report back at a certain time (use military time if you like) and be ready to share their information with the rest of the group.
6. When participants return, have them share information one by one. You can record this information on a flipchart and, in time, certain patterns should emerge.
7. Award each participant with a chocolate medallion for a job well done and do a quick debrief of the activity.

Guidelines for playing

*   Keep the activity moving quickly. The goal is to raise awareness of overt and covert organizational culture, not to learn everything possible about that culture.
*   For a larger group, send the participants in pairs to save time on the reporting back to the group.

Debriefing

QUESTIONS FOR THE DEBRIEF

1. What happened? What was easy to observe? What was not?
2. Why is it important to be aware of covert culture?

POINTS TO BRING FORTH IN THE DEBRIEF

*   All organizations have overt and covert culture. Being aware of both can be very helpful.

© Susan El-Shamy, *Dynamic Induction*, Gower Publishing Limited, 2003

Variations

- For a companion activity, review the written rules of conduct for the workplace, then generate and discuss some of the unwritten rules. Ask the new person to do a bit of reconnaissance in the workplace and gather information about unwritten rules.

31. What To Do

Overview

PURPOSE

To acquaint participants with the rules and regulations regarding days off, vacation time, sick time, and emergencies.

SUMMARY

Participants review basic information regarding time off, hours, sick leave, and emergencies by taking an open-book (employee handbook) fill-in-the-blank quiz.

MATERIALS

Copies of the employee handbook or other appropriate printed materials; copies of the quiz; small wrapped sweets or little packets of sweets or nuts to use for prizes.

TIME

20 minutes.

GROUP SIZE

Any size.

Before the game

Go through your employee handbook or other materials and gather information concerning work hours, time off, sick leave and emergencies. Put together a short fill-in-the-blank quiz that covers some of the most basic policies. For example, you might want to use items like:

1. If two or more employees request time off for the same time period, and the department's staffing needs do not allow both employees to be off, _____ is given preference.
2. If adverse weather creates extreme travel hazards for an employee travelling to or from the workplace, then the employee should _____.
3. Paid Time Off (PTO) benefits provide time off for vacation, sick leave, funeral attendance, and _____.

Choose information that you feel is most important for new employees to know, information that covers the most typical questions that new employees bring to their supervisors or the human resources department. Get input from people in human resources. What are the ten most frequently asked questions by new employees regarding time off, vacations, and so forth?

As you construct the quiz, keep in mind that you will be reading this quiz out loud. Have employee handbooks or other printed materials available for all participants and copies of the quiz to be distributed at the end of the exercise.

Opening lines

How many of you have ever taken an 'open-book test?' That's what we are going to do now. The book you will open is your employee handbook!

How to play the game

1. Distribute the employee handbooks or other printed materials and give the participants a minute or two to look through them.
2. Tell participants that you will be reading the test questions out loud and when the participants find the answer, they should raise their hands.
3. Call on the first person to raise their hand to give the answer and if it is right, give them a prize.
4. Continue through the quiz letting participants find the answers and giving prizes to people with correct answers.
5. When you've gone through all the questions, distribute copies of the quiz to everyone. See if they can remember all the correct answers without looking in their employee handbooks.
6. Conduct a short debrief of the activity.

Guidelines for playing

• Keep it lively and fun. Have a bowl of prizes sitting on the front table. As you read a question, reach in and pull out a prize and have it ready to toss when the right answer comes.

Debriefing

QUESTIONS FOR THE DEBRIEF

1. What happened? How likely were the situations?
2. What did you learn?

POINTS TO BRING FORTH IN THE DEBRIEF

• When in doubt about what to do, ask!

Variations

- Take this open-book fill-in-the-blank test with your induction companion. Use it as a stimulus for a discussion of time off, work hours, sick leave, and emergencies.

32. All for You

Overview

PURPOSE

To acquaint participants with the various services and assistance available to them in the organization.

SUMMARY

Participants generate a quick list of the names of people, departments, and services that they think they might need; participants win a prize for any names not on the list the instructor has prepared. The instructor then either immediately looks up the names in a company directory or agrees to get it to everyone in the next two days.

MATERIALS

Handouts with information on various agencies and services available to participants in the organization; prizes.

TIME

15–20 minutes.

GROUP SIZE

Any size.

Before the game

Prepare a list with the names, phone numbers, and e-mail addresses of various resource and assistance people, departments, agencies and services available to employees in the organization. Make more than enough copies needed and have them nearby.

Opening lines

Did any of you know that our organization has a travel office that can get you discounts on cinema tickets?

How to play the game

1. Explain that there are a number of services available to employees of the organization and say that you are interested in hearing from them what kind of information they would like to have regarding such services.
2. Let the group generate services that they would like to know about and list them on the flipchart.
3. When the group is done, take out the handout that you have prepared and tell them that if there are any items on their list that you do not have on your list, you will give them a prize and find the information for them.
4. Distribute the handout and go through the items listed there. Mark off items on the flipchart as they are covered in the handout. For items left on the flipchart, distribute some type of group prize (something that can easily be shared by all).
5. Look up any information that you can access immediately and share it with the group. Any information that you cannot find, tell them that you will send it to them later.
6. Do a quick debrief.

Debriefing

QUESTIONS FOR THE DEBRIEF

1. Were there any services that surprised you?
2. Why does the organization offer services and assistance?
3. Which of the services do you think you will use?

POINTS TO BRING FORTH IN THE DEBRIEF

- A healthy, happy, well-functioning employee is a benefit to the organization.
- These services are readily available and they should feel free to use them.

Variations

- For a companion activity, explain that there are a number of services available to employees of the organization and have the new employee generate a list of what kind of information he or she would like to have regarding such services. Then take out the handout and see how many are there. Discuss the services and together get information on any services that the new person is interested in but are not on the list.

33. Employee Development Opportunities

Overview

PURPOSE

To acquaint participants with the training, education and various employee development opportunities available to them through the organization.

SUMMARY

Participants form small groups that compete to complete a training and education questionnaire.

MATERIALS

Copies of the questionnaire; copies of the training and education manual; brochures and pamphlets from local education and training institutions; prizes.

TIME

20–30 minutes.

GROUP SIZE

Any size.

Before the game

Gather copies of the organization's training and education manual, brochures and pamphlets and manuals from local education institutions.
Make copies of the questionnaire on page 151 or construct your own similar questionnaire and make copies of it.

Opening lines

Have any of you seen a copy of our training manual? (Hold up a copy.)

How to play the game

1. Distribute copies of the organization's training manual and point out the other educational information on a back table.

2. Explain that you would like them to become better acquainted with the organization's training and education policies; to help them do this, you have a little questionnaire for them to fill in.
3. After the moaning and groaning, explain that they will be doing this in small teams and that there are rewards for completing the task!
4. Divide them into small groups of four to six people and give each group a questionnaire.
5. Tell them that they have fifteen minutes to complete all the items and bring their questionnaires to you. When they do so, you will give them a prize. After you give them a prize, let them keep their questionnaires to share with the whole class later.
6. When the time is up, have the groups reconvene into one large group again and go over their answers to the questionnaire.
7. Conduct a short debrief.

Guidelines for playing

- If there are limited copies of any of the material, make sure it is shared.

Debriefing

QUESTIONS FOR THE DEBRIEF

1. What happened? What did you find?
2. What programmes seemed most popular?
3. Was there anything that surprised you?

POINTS TO BRING FORTH IN THE DEBRIEF

- Employee development is good for the employee and the organization.

Variations

- For a companion activity, look through the organization's training and education manual with the new person. Then go over the training and development questionnaire with them. Share information about some of the training you have taken and encourage the new person to take advantage of the organization's educational opportunities.

The Questionnaire

1. What type of training programmes are available through the organization's training department?

2. If each of you had to choose one programme to attend from those listed in the manual, who would choose what?

3. Where are the organization's training programmes held?

4. Name three local institutions that offer technical training classes.

5. Describe the most unusual or unique class you were able to find.

6. What is the organization's policy on reimbursement of tuition fees?

7. Where can you get more information on employee development and training and education?

Understanding the Organization

34. Once Upon a Time

Overview

PURPOSE

To acquaint the participants with company history.

SUMMARY

Participants listen to a story of how the company started. There are occasional words missing from the story and participants write down what they think the missing words are. The participant with the highest number of correct answers for the missing words wins a prize.

MATERIALS

Handouts with a short history of the company; prizes.

TIME

15–20 minutes.

GROUP SIZE

Any size.

Before the game

Put together a handout consisting of a few paragraphs describing the origins of the organization or the early history of the company. For example:

Once upon a time there was a man named 1. _____ who worked for the 2. _____ company in 3. _____. At the age of 4. _____ he decided to leave 5. _____ company and begin his own company manufacturing 6. _____. With only 7. _____ pounds in the bank, but a lot of 8. _____ in his 9. _____, he rented a small warehouse on 10. _____ Street, recruited two production people and began what was then called 11. _____ company.

Make copies of the handout to have for participants.

Go through your copy of the handout and mark eight to twelve key words that you can leave out when you read it to the class. Number the words so that when you read it out loud instead of the words you can read the numbers.

Opening lines

How many of you are familiar with the history of our organization? I'd like to read a short description of how our company started. However, this copy has a few blanks. I'm going to ask you to fill in the blanks!

How to play the game

1. Distribute pencils and paper and ask participants to number their papers from one to however many blanks you have in the handout.
2. Tell them that when you get to a blank in the description, you will read out the number for that blank and they should write on the paper the word that they think is missing.
3. Read the history, pausing a moment at each numbered blank. When you are finished, ask the participants to exchange papers and score each other's papers.
4. Go through the history soliciting correct answers for the blanks and giving correct answers when necessary.
5. Award prizes to the three highest scores and give a consolation prize to the lowest score.
6. Go through a final version of the history reading into it the worst answers for the blanks.
7. Do a quick debrief.

Guidelines for playing

- Give the history a dramatic reading particularly when you read the version with the worst answers.

Debriefing

QUESTIONS FOR THE DEBRIEF

1. What happened?
2. Why do organizations like to share their history?
3. Why did I share this history with you today?

POINTS TO BRING FORTH IN THE DEBRIEF

- We are all a part of this organization and we all contribute to its history.

35. Where in the World is ...?

Overview

PURPOSE

To acquaint participants of large, national or international organizations with the various locations of the organization.

SUMMARY

Participants receive a list of company locations and have a limited time to find the locations and mark them with coloured pins on a large map.

MATERIALS

Large maps of the world, the country, the region and/or the city; coloured pins; prizes.

TIME

20 minutes.

GROUP SIZE

6–20 participants.

Before the game

If your company or organization is international, you will need a world map, a country map, a regional map and a city map. If it is a national company, you will need a country map, a regional map and a local, city map. If your company has locations only in the local area or city, then you will need only local area and/or city maps.

Put together lists of company locations. For international, put the names of countries; for national put the names of cities; and for local, list the addresses.

Post a large sign that says, 'Where in the World is _____ [Your Company Name]?' on one of the walls, and post the maps along that wall.

Opening lines

How many of you have been to other company locations? How many locations does our company have?

How to play the game

1. Divide the participants into as many groups as there are maps that you are using. If you are using only a local or regional map, have three copies of the map posted and divide the participants into three groups.
2. Tell them they have ten minutes to find and mark on their map all the locations on the list you will give them. When any group finishes, they should turn and help the other groups finish. If the whole class gets done in ten minutes of less, everyone will win a prize!
3. Distribute the appropriate lists and let the fun begin. If it becomes obvious that ten minutes will not be enough, allow them another five minutes.
4. When time is up, have everyone look over all the locations, distribute prizes and do a quick debrief.

Guidelines for playing

* Keep it quick and lively. Encourage cooperation.

Debriefing

QUESTIONS FOR THE DEBRIEF

1. What happened? Which places were most difficult to find?
2. Was it easy to help each other?
3. Why did I have you do this activity?

POINTS TO BRING FORTH IN THE DEBRIEF

* We are all part of a large organization and we will often need to work together to get the job done.

Variations

* This makes a nice companion activity. Spread the maps out on a table or hang them on a wall. Give the new person a list of company locations and a specific amount of time to find the locations and mark them with coloured pins. If they can find them all, you pay for refreshments.

36. The Big Picture Frame

Overview

PURPOSE

To provide participants with a visual overview of how the organization is structured.

SUMMARY

While the facilitator reads a description of how the organization is structured, the participants attempt to draw an organizational chart. Participants are then put into small groups where they share and combine their charts and produce a final organizational chart. Their chart is then compared to the official organizational chart.

MATERIALS

Copies of the official organizational chart; large sheets of white paper; coloured pens; prizes.

TIME

20 minutes.

GROUP SIZE

Any size.

Before the game

Get copies of the most recent official organizational chart. Write a short narrative that describes the chart (i.e., The company is headed by the Central Office which is headed by the president of the company and three senior vice-presidents, one each for finance, manufacturing and sales.) Test the narrative on a friend or two in the office. See how easy or difficult it is for them to draw an organizational chart and adjust your narrative accordingly.

Opening lines

How many of you are familiar with organizational charts? Have you seen one for this organization? Just in case you haven't, I've got copies of our current organizational chart for all of you. But before I distribute them, I'd like to try something.

How to play the game

1. Distribute blank paper to the participants and ask them to listen to your description of how the organization is structured and sketch out an organizational chart accordingly.
2. Read the description slowly and give them a bit of time to draw their charts.
3. Divide them into small groups of three to five people and let them share and compare their charts.
4. Read through your description once more, then ask each group to draw up a final organizational chart.
5. When their final charts are finished, post them on the wall and distribute the actual chart. Let the participants share and compare all the charts and decide which ones are more like the official one and award prizes accordingly.
6. Conduct a short debrief.

Guidelines for playing

• Make the activity quick and humorous.

Debriefing

QUESTIONS FOR THE DEBRIEF

1. What happened? How similar were your charts?
2. Why do this exercise?
3. Why is an organizational chart important?

POINTS TO BRING FORTH IN THE DEBRIEF

• Being aware of organizational structure, or the big picture, can give you a sense of where you fit in and how the larger organization works.

Variations

• Do a blindfolded version! Have one person from each team draw the organizational chart on a flipchart while they are blindfolded and you read the description.
• Deliberately make the narrative tricky with comments like, 'Oh, I almost forgot, there's an external relations office that also reports to the Central Office.'
• For a companion activity, read the description of how the organization is structured and let the new person attempt to draw an organizational chart. Then compare their chart to the official organizational chart and discuss organizational structure.

     © Susan El-Shamy, *Dynamic Induction*, Gower Publishing Limited, 2003

37. What We Are Famous For

Overview

PURPOSE

To acquaint participants with leading products and/or services of the organization.

SUMMARY

Participants try to match the names of products and services with their pictures and/or descriptions.

MATERIALS

Handouts; prizes.

TIME

20 minutes.

GROUP SIZE

Any size.

Before the game

Put together a handout with pictures and/or descriptions of a dozen or so organizational products and/or services at the top of the page. At the bottom of the handout, list the names of those products or services. Mix in a few extra names to make things fun. Make copies of the handout for all participants, plus another dozen or so extra.

Make a large poster-sized copy of the handout to use during this activity and post it after you distribute the handout.

Opening lines

How many of you remember taking tests in school? Did you ever have a teacher tell you 'Keep your eyes on your own paper. No cheating!' I have a short test for you to take right now, but let's try something. If you get to a question and you don't know the answer, I'd like you to look over at your neighbour's paper and see what they have put down. Borrow their answers if you like. OK?

How to play the game

1. Put up the poster of the products and services, then distribute the handout.
2. Tell participants they have five minutes to match the products/services with their names.
3. When time is up, have the participants form groups of three and share and compare their answers. Give each group of three a fresh handout and let them mark their final answers in the match up.
4. Go through the handout soliciting correct answers from the group.
5. Award prizes to the groups with all the correct answers.
6. Conduct a short debrief.

Debriefing

QUESTIONS FOR THE DEBRIEF

1. What happened? Which ones were easy? Which were hard?
2. Why do you need to know about these key products/services?

POINTS TO BRING FORTH IN THE DEBRIEF

• You will now be seen by many people as a representative of this organization and people will expect you to have knowledge of the products and services of the organization.

Variations

• As a companion activity, give the new person the handout and ask him or her to match the names of products and services with their pictures and/or descriptions, then, go over the answers. Use this activity to stimulate a discussion of products and services of the organization.

38. Who's Who?

Overview

PURPOSE

To acquaint new employees with some of the leaders of the organization.

SUMMARY

Participants try to match pictures of organizational leaders with descriptions of those leaders.

MATERIALS

Handouts; prizes.

TIME

20–30 minutes.

GROUP SIZE

Any size.

Before the game

Decide which organizational leaders to include in this activity. If your inductees come from all parts of the organization, you will want pictures of top management, the leaders of the various departments represented in your group, and a few other key figures in the organization; maybe the employee who has been with the organization the longest, employees who have recently won awards, and so forth. If possible, try to get candid shots from newsletters and websites.

Arrange the pictures in some creative manner (montage, chequerboard, pyramid) across the top of the page and number the pictures. The bottom half of the page can have short two- to three-sentence descriptions of the various people pictured. Mix the descriptions and put two or three blank spaces in front of each. Include a picture of yourself and a humorous description!

Make copies of the handout and have it at hand.

Opening lines

Have any of you ever had the opportunity to look at police mug-shots? This next activity may have similar overtones.

How to play the game

1. Distribute the handout and explain that each picture has a description of that person among the descriptions at the bottom of the page. All they have to do is find it!
2. Let people work in groups of three. Give them ten minutes to put the number of the pictures in the blanks before their descriptions.
3. When time is up, go through the pictures one by one getting input from the group and giving the correct answers.
4. Give prizes to participants with the highest scores and do a quick debrief.

Guidelines for playing

- Avoid unflattering photos and unflattering commentary!

Debriefing

QUESTIONS FOR THE DEBRIEF

1. What happened? Which photos were easy to identify? Why?
2. How did you decide who's who when you had no idea?
3. If we had a photo of you, what would the description say?
4. Why did we do this activity?

POINTS TO BRING FORTH IN THE DEBRIEF

- It never hurts to know who's who in the organization.

Variations

- Instead of handouts, have a large poster on the wall and have the class work together to match the descriptions with the pictures.
- Do a handout of class participant pictures and descriptions and do this activity early in the programme as a get-acquainted activity.
- For a companion activity, give the new person the handout and ask them to try to match pictures of organizational leaders with descriptions of those leaders. Go over the right answers and discuss organizational leaders and some of the important leaders in your part of the organization.

39. The Teamwork Puzzle

Overview

PURPOSE

To acquaint participants with the basic principles of the organization's teamwork philosophy.

SUMMARY

Small groups of participants compete to put together jigsaw puzzles that present the organization's teamwork philosophy and programmes.

MATERIALS

Blank 12–20 piece jigsaw puzzles; prizes.

TIME

20–30 minutes.

GROUP SIZE

6–25.

Before the game

Prepare half a dozen blank jigsaw puzzles by putting information on them about your organization's teamwork philosophy. (You can often find blank jigsaw puzzles at teacher supply stores or art supply stores.) Do this by using some type of visual or written summary of your organization's philosophy. For example, if your organization has a particular slogan, logo, or numbered series of initiatives, you might try combining one of those with a sentence or two. In order to fill the entire area of the puzzle, you might want to add the name of the organization and other items.

Draw or print your final message onto blank pre-cut jigsaw puzzles. Try to arrange the material onto the puzzle in such a way as to make the puzzle difficult, but not too difficult!

Before the class, decide on how many puzzles you will be using, one for each small group of three to six participants. Take that number of puzzles and lay them out on a table. Take two key pieces from the first puzzle and set them on top of the second puzzle. Take two key pieces from the second puzzle (but different pieces from the first puzzle) and lay them on top of the third puzzle. Do this for as many puzzles as you have until you have taken two key pieces from the last puzzle and put them on top of the first puzzle.

Now, for each puzzle, take apart the remaining pieces and place them, along with the two borrowed pieces, into a separate plastic bag. You should finally have a plastic bag for each puzzle. Each plastic bag should contain all the pieces for that puzzle, minus two that have gone into another bag, and plus two additional pieces that have come from another puzzle.

Have copies of company materials on teamwork that you can distribute after this game.

Opening lines

How many of you are familiar with our teamwork programme?

How to play the game

1. Divide the participants into small groups of three to six people. Explain that they will be putting together jigsaw puzzles that have information printed on them about teamwork in the organization.
2. Give each group a plastic bag containing a puzzle.
3. Explain that they will have ten minutes to put their puzzle together. Any group that completes the puzzle in less than ten minutes will win a prize.
4. Tell the group that once they begin working on their puzzle you cannot help them or give them additional information. Then say 'You have ten minutes. Put your puzzles together.'
5. As the groups begin to realize that something is wrong with the puzzle, they will turn to you with questions and complaints. Your answer should be, 'I'm sorry the rules are that I can't give you any help or information. All I can tell you is put your puzzles together.'
6. Eventually, someone will get the idea of the groups working together and helping each other to find the missing pieces to their puzzles.
7. Distribute prizes as groups complete their puzzles.
8. When all the puzzles have been put together, explain that we may all work in small teams most of the time, but we are all part of the larger team all of the time!
9. Conduct a short debrief.

Guidelines for playing

*   If time is running out and it looks as if no one will get the idea of helping each other, you can give clues like 'What is the name of this game?' or 'What does it say so far on the pieces that you have put together?'

Debriefing

QUESTIONS FOR THE DEBRIEF

1. What happened?
2. How did it feel when you realized you didn't have all of the pieces that you needed?
3. What did you learn from this game?

POINTS TO BRING FORTH IN THE DEBRIEF

*   We are all part of the biggest team of all – the organization.
*   Within the organization you are a part of many teams, but ultimately, we are all on the same team.

Variations

*   For classes of six or fewer participants, let individuals try to solve their own puzzles then get help from one another.

40. Quality and Customer Service Game

Overview

PURPOSE

To acquaint the participants with the organization's quality and customer service programmes.

SUMMARY

Participants are sent on an information hunt and must bring back information, materials, samples, examples, and so forth about the organization's quality and customer service programmes.

MATERIALS

None.

TIME

45 minutes.

GROUP SIZE

Any size.

Before the game

Become familiar with where information and materials on quality and customer service are available just in case you need to help participants find some!

Opening lines

Are any of you familiar with our organization's quality programme? How about our customer service programme? This next activity will help you become even more familiar!

How to play the game

1. Tell participants that they are about to embark on an information hunt that will be followed by an entertaining show-and-tell opportunity.

2. Divide participants into two groups, the quality group and the customer service group. For a larger number of people, you might want to have two quality and two customer service groups.
3. Tell them they will have fifteen minutes in which to gather information and artefacts on their topic from around the workplace and then prepare an entertaining show-and-tell presentation for the rest of the group. Explain that they should try to get informational material to share and artefacts (objects made by human beings; posters, logos, slogans, etc.) and that by entertaining show and tell you mean a presentation that is humorous, musical, and/or artistic.
4. On a flipchart write, 'Showtime will be at ...' and give a time fifteen minutes away.
5. Let the groups give their entertaining show-and-tell presentations and conduct a short debrief of the activity.

Guidelines for playing

- Have a few props available to help in the preparations of entertaining presentations – a box with scarves, hats, ribbons, an umbrella, coloured paper, scissors and tape.

Debriefing

QUESTIONS FOR THE DEBRIEF

1. What happened?
2. How did you decide what to do?
3. What did you learn?

POINTS TO BRING FORTH IN THE DEBRIEF

- It's one thing to read about quality and customer service, it's quite another thing to demonstrate it.

41. TLAs Are Everywhere!

Overview

PURPOSE

To acquaint participants with some of the three-letter abbreviations (TLAs) that are commonly used in the organization.

SUMMARY

Participants try to match a number of common three-letter abbreviations with the words that they stand for.

MATERIALS

Handouts of three-letter abbreviations and their possible meanings.

TIME

15–20 minutes.

GROUP SIZE

Any size.

Before the game

Prepare a handout of frequently used three-letter abbreviations. You may also include a few FLAs if you have them (four- and five-letter abbreviations). Put the abbreviations across the top of the paper in large print and list a number of possible meanings across the bottom. Include a number of plausible wrong answers and a few absurd answers too!

Opening lines

How many of you know what a TLA is? It's a three-letter abbreviation, like TCS for total customer satisfaction or SPC for statistical process control. All organizations have TLAs and right now we're going to look at some of the more popular TLAs in our organizaion. Maybe even a couple of FLAs!

How to play the game

1. Distribute the handouts. Tell participants that they can work in pairs if they like.
2. Tell people they will have five minutes to draw lines connecting the TLAs to their right meanings.

© Susan El-Shamy, *Dynamic Induction*, Gower Publishing Limited, 2003

3. When time is up, go through the TLAs and give the right meanings. Present prizes to all participants who got them all right.

Debriefing

QUESTIONS FOR THE DEBRIEF

1. What happened? Which were easy? Which were difficult?
2. Why do organizations have so many TLAs?

POINTS TO BRING FORTH IN THE DEBRIEF

- TLAs are helpful as a shorthand system for handling long, repetitive phrases. They also serve as a group cohesion mechanism. Only the insiders know what the letters stand for!

Variations

- As a companion activity, give the new person the handout and let them try to match the three-letter abbreviations with the words that they stand for. Use this activity to stimulate a discussion of TLAs and why organizations always have them!

42. Company Quiz Bowl

Overview

PURPOSE

To acquaint participants with basic information about the organization.

SUMMARY

Participants quickly review a variety of information about the company before taking part in a quiz bowl about the organization.

MATERIALS

Lists of questions and answers about the organization; a bell or buzzer; items with the company logo on them to use as prizes.

TIME

30–60 minutes.

GROUP SIZE

6–18.

Before the game

Using the organization's annual report, a general brochure about the organization, and the employee handbook, put together a list of basic questions and answers about the organization. Include questions such as what year the company was founded, the name of the person currently heading the organization, the approximate number of current employees, the mission statement, and so forth.

You will need fifteen basic questions and six difficult questions. Put the questions on 3 x 5 cards. Set the six difficult questions aside to be used in the event of a tie and shuffle the remaining fifteen cards to be used in the game. Set them where you can find them easily when it's time for the game.

Have enough copies of the materials you used for the list of questions and answers on hand to distribute to participants during this activity.

Opening lines

How many of you like to watch quiz shows? Has anyone ever participated in a quiz show? Well, we're going to conduct our own little quiz show right now.

How to play the game

1.   Divide the participants into three teams. Ask each team to give itself a name.
2.   List the team names on a flipchart and explain that you will be keeping score on the flipchart.
3.   Distribute the handbooks, brochures, annual reports and whatever other information you have to each of the teams. Tell them that they will have ten minutes to divide the information among themselves and review it as best they can. When the ten minutes are up, they will set the information aside and the quiz bowl will begin.
4.   After ten minutes, collect the information and explain how the quiz bowl will work.
     *   Each team should choose a spokesperson to give the answers to the questions.
     *   When the facilitator asks a question, the team will have thirty seconds to decide upon a response. At the end of the thirty seconds, the facilitator will ring the bell (or hit the gong, or blow the whistle, or sound the buzzer) and the team spokesperson must answer.
     *   Five points will be given for each right answer, two points for a partially right answer and no points for a wrong answer. The facilitator will determine the points to be awarded.
     *   One by one, each team will be asked a question and given 30 seconds to decide on a response.
     *   There are five rounds of questions and answers, at the end of which the scores will be totalled and the winners determined.
5.   Conduct the five rounds of questions. After asking a question, wait thirty seconds then ring a bell (or hit the gong or whatever) and ask for their answer. Award five points for each correct answer and two points for partially correct answers. Keep score on a flipchart.
6.   When all fifteen questions have been answered, check the scores for a winner. If there is a tie, have the tied teams compete until a winner emerges or simply award prizes to both teams.
7.   Conduct a short debrief.

Guidelines for playing

*   Let teams make up mascots, slogans and/or logos to go with their names and put them on posters to hang on the wall behind their team.

173

Debriefing

QUESTIONS FOR THE DEBRIEF

1. What happened?
2. Why did we play this game?
3. How will you use any of the information you obtained?

POINTS TO BRING FORTH IN THE DEBRIEF

- You are now a part of this organization and may need to know some of this information in the near future.

Variations

- The whole quiz bowl could be made into an e-game and put onto the induction website.

43. The Company Board Game

Overview

PURPOSE

To help new employees learn a variety of information about the organization.

SUMMARY

Participants play a board game to learn about the organization. Small groups of three to four participants sit around game boards, draw cards, answer questions, roll dice and move tokens around the board. The cards contain questions and answers about the company and its products, services, and programmes.

MATERIALS

Copies of the Company Board game; prizes.

TIME

45 minutes.

GROUP SIZE

4–30.

Before the game

This game will take a lot of preparation, but it can be worth it. Although there is a fair amount of time and effort that goes into preparing the board game, once it is done it can be easily updated and used over a long period of time. Participants react very positively to board games because they are fun and involving.

The amount of information covered in the game can vary greatly, although a great deal of information can be covered in a reasonable amount of time. You might want to design the game to deal with very specific organizational information or you might decide to extend the content to cover all aspects of the organization: its history, structure, major products and services, and so on.

Using a basic game board model, such as that on page 179, you can add your own organizational logo, the name of your organization and any interesting graphics you like. Prepare a stack of question and answer cards following the suggestions below. You will need a game board, a stack of cards, a die and tokens for every four players.

You can choose between two types of cards, basic question cards or multiple choice question cards. Basic question cards contain questions about the subject matter. For example, a card deck could contain questions about the history of the organization: 'When was the organization founded?' or 'Who was the first President?' Or, you might have questions about products and services such as 'What is the name of our best-selling mystery novel this year?' or 'Who is the author of our current best-selling spy novel?' The answers should be written on the card beneath the question. The opponent draws a card and asks the other player the question. If the player gets it right, they can roll the die and move that number of squares forward. If they get it wrong, they have to stay where they are, or, as a variation, have them take two steps back!

For multiple-choice question cards, the cards have the question, the choices, and the answer all on the front of the card. The opponent draws the card and quizzes the player. For example, a card containing a question about the history of the organization might read, 'When was the organization founded? (a) 1710, (b) 1808, (c) 1901 or (d) 1937?' If the player gives the right answer, they roll the die and move that many squares forward. If they get it wrong, they have to stay where they are.

If you have four people or fewer playing at each game board, and it takes each person at least four and probably six rolls of the die before someone reaches the finishing line, then you will need at least 25 cards, probably 30 or more to be safe. If the most any one player can roll on any one turn is six, and you want each player to have at least three turns, then you will need at least 30 spaces. If your board has fewer than 30 spaces, say between 15 and 25, then you will want to add a few special squares, such as 'Sorry! Move two steps back!' You can also make a couple of Joker cards and when a player draws a Joker, they have to move back so many spaces. And, as mentioned earlier, you can add a rule that when a player misses a question, he or she has to take two steps back.

Most board games use dice or a spinner to determine movement. These can be purchased at game stores, teacher supply houses or large discount stores. Using a single die is most effective for small game boards that have two to four players. One die will limit the number of spaces a player can move forward and therefore you can use a smaller game board.

You will need to write out directons for playing the game and distribute them to the players. Also, each player will need an object to move around the board. This can be a coin, a plastic pawn, or even a wrapped sweet. When it is a player's turn, one of the opponents draws a card and reads the question. If the player answers correctly, they roll the die and move ahead the number of spaces on the die. Play continues until one player at each game board wins, or until all players at all game boards reach the finish square. (You may want to set a time limit.) See how many players can reach the finish square in twenty minutes or some such time.

You will also need prizes, preferably ones that can be easily shared.

Opening lines

How many of you like to play board games? Scrabble, Monopoly, Trivial Pursuit? We have a special company board game for you to play right now. Let me tell you about it.

How to play the game

1. Divide the participants into groups of three or four players and give each group a game board. Pass around sample cards until each participant has one.
2. Distribute the handout on how to play the game and go over the rules and guidelines with them. Have them look at the sample card. Tell them they will soon get a whole stack of cards and the game will begin.
3. See if there are any questions. Make sure everyone understands how to play the game.
4. Give each group a stack of cards, a die and tokens. Explain that they have 30 minutes to see how many of them can win in that time.
5. Give a five-minute warning. Encourage groups without winners to play these last five minutes very quickly.
6. When time is up, stop the game and pass out prizes.
7. Ask the participants to look quickly through any remaining cards that they haven't read. See if there are any comments or questions on the game.
8. Conduct a short debrief.

Guidelines for playing

• Monitor the groups to keep play going at a good pace. Lengthy discussions can cause some groups to have no winners!

Debriefing

QUESTIONS FOR THE DEBRIEF

1. What happened? How did you like the game?
2. Which questions were most difficult?
3. What did you learn?

POINTS TO BRING FORTH IN THE DEBRIEF

- It can be very helpful to know quite a bit about the organization!

Variations

- This can make a fun companion activity. Let the new employee know when they will be playing the game so he or she can study up on the organization. Then, when you play the game, if the new person beats the companion, the companion has to take the new person out to lunch.

START →	Go ahead two spaces!				
FINISH					Go back three spaces!
					Go ahead two spaces!
Go back three spaces!					
	Go ahead two spaces!				Go back three spaces!

You and Your Job

Adjusting to the New Position

44. Where Do You Fit In?

Overview

PURPOSE

To give participants a feel for where they are within the organization.

SUMMARY

Participants determine where they fall within a large organizational chart and then try to place a sticker with their name on it in the right location on the chart while blindfolded. Participants whose stickers come closest to where they really belong win prizes. Participants also look for links that they have with other participants.

MATERIALS

Large copy of the organizational chart; small stickers; two or three blindfolds; copies of class list with participants' names and e-mail numbers.

TIME

15 minutes.

GROUP SIZE

Twenty or less.

Before the game

Get a copy of the current organizational chart and make a large, poster-sized copy of it. Also make copies of the class list with the names and e-mail addresses of all participants. Have two or three blindfolds ready to use for this game; scarves will work nicely.

Opening lines

How many of you have a pretty good sense of where you are located within the larger organization? For those of you who haven't, maybe this activity will help.

How to play the game

1. Post the large organizational chart and ask the participants to come up to the chart and point out to one another where they fall within the chart.

2. Distribute small stickers and ask each participant to take one and write their name on it. Have the participants number off and then stand in line starting with number one.
3. Ask the first two or three people in line to put on blindfolds. One by one, have the blindfolded participants stand three feet in front of the chart, then walk up to the chart and put their sticker where they think it belongs.
4. When they finish, they can take off their blindfolds and give it to the next person in the line.
5. After all stickers have been stuck, the participants whose stickers have come closest to where they should be win prizes.
6. Conduct a short debrief.

Guidelines for playing

- Keep the game moving quickly.

Debriefing

QUESTIONS FOR THE DEBRIEF

1. What happened?
2. In what ways is playing this game like finding out where you are in the organization?

POINTS TO BRING FORTH IN THE DEBRIEF

- You may feel as if you are walking around blindly for a while in your new job, but eventually you will know your way and where you belong.

Variations

- Throw darts at the chart to see where people will end up in the organization.

45. What You Do and How You Do It

Overview

PURPOSE

To get participants thinking about their jobs and what they do and do not know about their jobs.

SUMMARY

Participants with very different types of jobs are paired and they describe to one another what they do in their job and how they do it. One partner asks questions until there is something about the other person's job that they do not know and need to find out about. Then they switch and the other partner asks questions until there is something about the first partner's job that they do not know and need to find out. This is done for ten minutes. The first five minutes are done verbally, the last five minutes non-verbally!

MATERIALS

Large index cards or pieces of thin card; markers.

TIME

20 minutes.

GROUP SIZE

Any size.

Before the game

No particular preparations are required before this activity.

Opening lines

How many of you have questions about your new job and exactly what you will be doing?

How to play the game

1. Distribute cards and markers to the participants and ask them to write their job titles on the cards.

2. Tell participants to stand, take their cards, and go to an open area in the room. Ask them to hold up their cards and mix and mingle for a minute or two looking at the various job titles in the room.

3. Ask participants to find a partner who has a job that is fairly different from their own. Once they are paired up, ask them to introduce themselves. If there are an odd number of participants, you can have one three-way pairing or you can participate with a partner if you like.

4. Ask the partners to assign themselves a letter: A or B. One of them is to be A and the other of them is to be B.

5. Begin with partner A asking partner B questions about their job until there is something about B's job that B does not know and needs to find out about. Then they switch and B asks questions until there is something about A's job that A does not know and needs to find out. This is done for five minutes.

6. After five minutes, stop the questioning for a moment and tell the participants that they must continue the activity for another five minutes; now, the person answering questions must do so non-verbally. That is, they cannot speak! They can answer using sign language, or pantomime, or perhaps even drawing their answers. But they may not speak!

7. When the last five minutes is up, call an end to the activity and have participants return to their seats.

8. Conduct a short debrief.

Guidelines for playing

• Keep it lively and informative. The goal is to learn about each other's jobs, not to trip each other up.

Debriefing

QUESTIONS FOR THE DEBRIEF

1. What happened? How did it feel to be questioned?
2. What did you learn?
3. Why did I ask you to do this activity?

POINTS TO BRING FORTH IN THE DEBRIEF

• We all have a lot to learn about our own jobs and the jobs of others.

46. Measuring Up

Overview

PURPOSE

To let participants consider the major competencies needed to do their jobs well and on what type of criteria they will be judged.

SUMMARY

Participants list the major competencies needed to do their jobs well and then assess themselves on those competencies. They also list the criteria they think will be used to judge their success at their jobs. Competencies and criteria are shared and compared and the group picks the top five competencies and criteria. Participants with the most matches of group criteria with their own criteria receive a prize.

MATERIALS

Blank flipchart pages; markers; tape; prizes.

TIME

30 minutes.

GROUP SIZE

5–25.

Before the game

Tear off a few blank flipchart pages and stack them nearby. Have plenty of coloured markers ready.

Opening lines

How many of you love performance appraisals and are looking forward to your first one on the new job? Let's spend some time looking at what is expected of you, what competencies you need to exhibit and what criteria will be used to assess your performance.

How to play the game

1. Have participants take out a piece of paper and list some of the major competencies needed to do their jobs well. Ask them to list five to ten competencies if they can.

2. Ask them to rate themselves on each competency; did well, need to improve, not sure.
3. Ask participants now to list the criteria they think will be used to judge their success at their jobs. (Measurements like amount of work done, quality of work, speed of work, and so forth.)
4. Have participants form small groups of three or four people and share and compare what they have written about competencies and criteria.
5. Ask each group to come up with five key competencies that all of them, or most of them, had on their lists.
6. Now have the small groups come up with five basic criteria that all or most of them had on their lists.
7. Distribute the flipchart paper and markers and ask each group to prepare two charts, one listing their five key competencies and one listing their five basic criteria.
8. Tell the groups to post their charts on the wall and have all of the participants stand in front of the charts and discuss and compare the contents.
9. Have the group come up with the top five competencies and the top five criteria for the group.
10. Ask participants to check their original, individual lists of competencies and criteria. Give a prize to participants with most of the top group competencies and criteria on their own original lists.
11 Suggest that participants make a note of questions they might have for their boss and colleagues, and issues to think about further.
12. Conduct a short debrief.

Guidelines for playing

• Keep it lively and moving quickly. It is easy for this activity to get bogged down in lengthy discussions and sharing of personal past experiences.

Debriefing

QUESTIONS FOR THE DEBRIEF

1. What happened? What did you learn?
2. What competencies do you need to improve?
3. Are there questions about competencies and criteria that you need to discuss with your supervisor or manager?

POINTS TO BRING FORTH IN THE DEBRIEF

• It is important to be aware of the competencies and criteria being used to evaluate your work.

Variations

- This activity can lead into a really good companion discussion. Have the new person list the major competencies needed to do their job well and then let them assess themselves on those competencies. They can also list the criteria they think will be used to judge their success at their job. Finally, discuss performance criteria and the type of performance feedback that the new person can expect.

47. The Good, the Bad and the Ugly

Overview

PURPOSE

To have participants consider what they like, don't like and don't know about their new jobs.

SUMMARY

This charades game has participants acting out the aspects they like, don't like, and don't know about their new jobs.

MATERIALS

None.

TIME

30 minutes.

GROUP SIZE

6–24.

Before the game

No preparation is necessary.

Opening lines

How many of you have seen that old Clint Eastwood film, The Good, the Bad and the Ugly? This next activity is called the Good, the Bad and the Ugly and it looks at the things you like, don't like and don't know about your new jobs.

How to play the game

1. Tell the participants to consider their new jobs and what they like, don't like and don't know about the job. Explain that they will be acting out those three aspects and seeing if others can guess what they are.
2. Divide the participants into groups of three and ask them to assign themselves as A, B, and C.

3. Tell them that they will each have three minutes to act out their 'good, bad and ugly'. A will go first, then B, and then C. You will time the exercise and say, 'Go' when it is A's turn and 'Stop' when the three minutes are up. Then do the same for B and C.

4. When they finish, ask each group to choose someone to participate in a charades playoff. The chosen participants then act out their good, bad and ugly charades for the whole group.

5. After the playoff charades are over, let the group choose three winners: the best, the worst and the ugliest!

6. Conduct a short debrief.

Guidelines for playing

• Keep it quick and low key. Encourage participants to discuss why they chose as they did.

Debriefing

QUESTIONS FOR THE DEBRIEF

1. What happened? Why did we use charades?
2. What did you learn?
3. How will you use what you learned?

POINTS TO BRING FORTH IN THE DEBRIEF

• All jobs have aspects we like, aspects we don't like and areas of the unknown.

48. Now, Then and Some Day

Overview

PURPOSE
To have participants think about their career future.

SUMMARY
Participants write down the answers to three questions about where they are right now in their careers and what they are doing, where they would like to be in two or three years and what they would like to be doing, and where they would like to be and what they would like to be doing some day.

MATERIALS
Handouts; crystal ball or an eight-sided novelty crystal ball that produces stock answers such as 'not likely' and 'yes, if you work hard' when you turn over to a new side.

TIME
20 minutes.

GROUP SIZE
Any size.

Before the game
Find a novelty item crystal ball that produces different answers when it is turned over. The answers are usually phrases like 'good chance', 'will never happen', 'it will take a long time', and '50–50 chance'.

Opening lines
How many of you have an idea of what you would like to be doing five years from now in terms of work, job, and career?

How to play the game
1. Tell the participants that this activity will ask them to consider their present job and their future career. Ask them to take out a piece of paper and answer the three questions you will ask.

2. Ask the following three questions giving people time to write down their responses:
    *   Where are you right now in your career and what kind of work are you doing?
    *   Where would you like to be in your career two or three years from now and what would you like to be doing?
    *   Where would you like to be in your career and what would you like to be doing some day?
3. Tell participants to get a partner, preferably someone they have not talked to yet in the programme. Have the partners discuss their responses to the items on the handout.
4. Ask participants why it is important to think ahead about their careers. Ask how the new jobs they are just beginning will affect their future career.
5. Now tell the participants to write down one key question that they have about their future careers. Give examples like, 'Will I be rich and famous?' or 'Will I own my own company?'
6. Pull out the crystal ball and set it on the table in front of the participants. Then, one by one, have them ask their questions and you find the answers in the crystal ball.
7. Conduct a short debrief.

Debriefing

QUESTIONS FOR THE DEBRIEF

1. Why is it important to think about your long-term career just as you are starting a new job?
2. Why did I include the crystal ball activity?

POINTS TO BRING FORTH IN THE DEBRIEF

*   You can't always tell the future, but it helps to think ahead now and then.

Variations

*   For a companion activity, both the companion and the new person fill in the form and then talk about their career futures.

49. Putting It All Together

Overview

PURPOSE

To have participants summarize the induction workshop.

SUMMARY

Participants present a non-verbal summary of what they have learned in the induction programme.

MATERIALS

Props; coloured paper; markers; scissors.

TIME

30 minutes.

GROUP SIZE

6–30.

Before the game

Gather a few props to have available to help in the preparation of these non-verbal presentations – a box with scarves, hats, ribbons, items with the company logo, coloured paper, scissors and tape.

Opening lines

How many of you are familiar with the term 'non-verbal communication'? This final activity will call upon your talents for using non-verbal communication.

How to play the game

1. Divide the participants into groups of three to five people.
2. Tell them that their assignment is to prepare a short, one to three-minute creative presentation summarizing what they have learned from the induction workshop; inform participants that their presentation must be non-verbal. They can use written words, drawings, skits, and they can make noises, but no spoken words.
3. Tell them they have ten minutes to prepare and they may use any of the props and materials available in the room.

4. After ten minutes, announce, 'Showtime' and begin the presentations.
5. Conduct a short debrief.

Guidelines for playing

- Keep it lively. Encourage participants to have some fun and be a little crazy.

Debriefing

QUESTIONS FOR THE DEBRIEF

1. What happened? How did you decide what to do?
2. Why did I ask you to do this particular activity?

POINTS TO BRING FORTH IN THE DEBRIEF

- Fun and creativity can be an important component of the workplace.

50. Celebration Station

Overview

PURPOSE
To have participants celebrate their new jobs.

SUMMARY
Participants plan a final induction programme activity to celebrate their new jobs.

MATERIALS
Party hats; celebration supplies; gift items with organization logos.

TIME
30 minutes.

GROUP SIZE
6–24.

Before the game

Have ready one gift item for each participant. It is better if the gift item is something with the company logo or perhaps a product of the company. The gift can be as simple as a pen or pencil with the company logo.

Also have a box filled with party hats, noisemakers, balloons, and similar party items ready for participants to use.

Have some special refreshments ready for this activity. A cake with 'Congratulations' written on it works well.

Opening lines

How many of you celebrated after you heard that you got this job?

How to play the game

1. Explain to the participants that they will be planning a special celebration activity to celebrate their new jobs and to welcome them into the organization.
2. Tell the participants they will have fifteen minutes to plan a fifteen-minute activity. Show them the box of party items, the gifts, and the

refreshments. Also volunteer to help in any way that you can. Offer to be the master of ceremonies for the event.

3.   When the time is up, let the participants explain how they would like the celebration activity to happen; help them make it happen! Do everything you can to make it fun. If and when you present the gifts, do so solemnly as a warm welcome into the organization.

4.   End the activity, and the programme, with lots of applause and general merriment. No debrief is needed.

Guidelines for playing

*   If participants ask for suggestions or examples of what they might do, here are a few:
    *   One by one the instructor calls out the names of the participants and they step forward to receive their gift and congratulatory applause from the group.
    *   Have a large poster that says something like 'Welcome Aboard!' and each new employee comes forward, signs on, shakes the instructor's hand and receives a gift. The poster could then be hung in some central area of the organization for the next week.

Debriefing

No debrief is necessary.

Index

Index